Dear
Black Girl

Dear Black Girl

Letters from your Sisters on Stepping into your power

TAMARA WINFREY HARRIS

BK

Berrett–Koehler Publishers, Inc.

Berrett-Koehler Publishers, Inc.
1333 Broadway, Suite 1000
Oakland, CA 94612-1921
Tel: (510) 817-2277
Fax: (510) 817-2278
www.bkconnection.com

ORDERING INFORMATION
Quantity sales. Special discounts are available on quantity purchases by corporations, associations, and others. For details, contact the "Special Sales Department" at the Berrett-Koehler address above.

Individual sales. Berrett-Koehler publications are available through most bookstores. They can also be ordered directly from Berrett-Koehler: Tel: (800) 929-2929; Fax: (802) 864-7626; www.bkconnection.com.

Orders for college textbook / course adoption use. Please contact Berrett-Koehler: Tel: (800) 929-2929; Fax: (802) 864-7626.

Distributed to the U.S. trade and internationally by Penguin Random House Publisher Services.

Berrett-Koehler and the BK logo are registered trademarks of Berrett-Koehler Publishers, Inc.

Printed in the United States of America

Berrett-Koehler books are printed on long-lasting acid-free paper. When it is available, we choose paper that has been manufactured by environmentally responsible processes. These may include using trees grown in sustainable forests, incorporating recycled paper, minimizing chlorine in bleaching, or recycling the energy produced at the paper mill.

Library of Congress Cataloging-in-Publication Data
Names: Winfrey Harris, Tamara, author.
Title: Dear Black girl : letters from your sisters on stepping into your power / Tamara Winfrey Harris.
Description: First edition. | Oakland, CA : Berrett-Koehler Publishers, [2021] | Includes index. | Summary: "From the bestselling author of The Sisters Are Alright comes a book of personal letters written by black women to black girls to nurture healthy womanhood and sisterhood, covering topics like identity, self-love, parents, violence, grief, mental health, sex, and sexuality"—Provided by publisher.
Identifiers: LCCN 2020044428 | ISBN 9781523092291 (paperback ; alk. paper) | ISBN 9781523092307 (adobe pdf) | ISBN 9781523092314 (epub)
Subjects: LCSH: African American girls—Life skills guides. | African American women— Social conditions. | Conduct of life. | Self-esteem in women. | Self-realization in women. | Stereotypes (Social psychology) | Racism.
Classification: LCC E185.86 .W5564 2021 | DDC 305.48/896073—dc23
LC record available at https://lccn.loc.gov/2020044428

First Edition
26 25 24 23 22 21   10 9 8 7 6 5 4 3 2 1

Book production and interior design by Happenstance Type-O-Rama
Cover designed by Mike Nicholls
Cover illustration by Monica Ahanonu

For Kennedy, Kya, Nina, and
Brooklyn—I am here for you. Always.
May I be successful in preparing the
world to accept your sparkling brilliance.
You deserve everything. I love you.

And for the Black girls who came before
me—Constance, Georgia, Ida, Mattie,
Josie, Maggie, Ella, and all I cannot
name. Because of you, I am.

To Mommy and Daddy—if this Black
girl makes you proud, I am happy.

CONTENTS

PREFACE

We Are Alright

My Black girls, you tell me things.

You tell me how you love your mamas, but kind of hate them, too.

You tell me about the "ugh, fuckboys" at school who text dirty messages.

You tell me about beauty insecurities—"too big" noses and "*five*heads."

You tell me who you like, showing me pictures of boys on IG and giggling, "Ain't he cute?"

You tell me these things and I smile.

It has been a while since I was a girl, but I remember hating my parents' rules and being insecure about my looks. I remember the trifling boys and superfine crushes. Some things about Black girlhood never change.

You tell me other things, too.

You tell me about anxiety or depression that will not let go.

You tell me about social media memes that leave you feeling demeaned and hated.

You tell me about boys and men who violate you and families who cannot deal with the devastation of sexual assault.

You tell me about carrying the burden of friends and family who have been murdered.

You tell me about families who cannot accept your queer identity.

You tell me about schools that suspend you for petty reasons.

You tell me how people assume you are angry, unfeminine, grown, and hypersexual—before you can even find out who you are for yourself.

You tell me these things and I worry.

I remember that the world does not value Black girls like it should. Some things that are too common in Black girlhood *must* change.

Black girl, the world looks at you with a white patriarchal gaze—a fixed, negative view that says whiteness and maleness are superior and valuable, while you—Black and a girl—are deficient. It makes your life harder. It makes my life harder, too. We are sisters in a unique struggle. Black women know the things you may experience when you are a Black girl. We have lived through many of them ourselves. Many of us have been told our skin is too dark, our hair is too short, or our noses are too big. Many of us have been sent out of classrooms—away from the education we desperately need. Many of us have difficult relationships with our mamas or daddies. Many of us have been called loud or "ghetto." Many of us have unchecked anxiety.

Many of us have lost friends to violence. Many of us have struggled to understand how our Blackness and girlhood intersect with our other identities. Many of us have walked down the street past men who say ugly things. We understand.

That is why something else that Black girls, like you, tell me breaks my heart.

You say that some Black women seem to have fixed, negative ideas about Black girls, too. It is too often Black women who say Black girls' hair is not fit for the classroom, Black women who fuss that Black girls are not "ladylike," Black women who complain about Black girls' "bad attitudes," Black women who expect Black girls to stare down depression, Black women who chastise Black girls about being "fast." You tell me it is too often Black women who reinforce the idea that you are deficient and of less value—angry, unfeminine, grown, and hypersexual—before you can even find out who you are for yourself.

My dearest Black girl, if this has been your experience, I am so sorry.

There are Black women in the world who love you fiercely. But many of us are still hurting from the ways we were treated as girls and young women. We do our best. We don't mean to sound like all those other people. We want desperately for our Black girls to be okay in this country that does not care much for Black people or girls. And sometimes our love gets twisted by the lies we've been told about ourselves and each other for too long.

What we really want to say to Black girls is, "I was once you. I know the world thinks every Black girl is a 'ho.' I want to protect you from that. I want you to make good decisions. I want you to be safe and happy. And I am scared for you." But too often, on the outside, our fear sounds like disgust: "Look at you out here being fast!"

If we want to live free and happy, Black women and Black girls must love each other well. We cannot afford to look on each other with the same eyes as those who hate us. Our gaze must be one of love, empathy, and acceptance for all Black girl identities and experiences.

More than a year ago, I asked some Black women on social media for twelve letters to give a group of Black girls in a workshop. I asked them to write letters that were loving, truthful, vulnerable, feminist, anti-racist, body positive, LGBTQ+ positive, anti-respectability politics, and pro-Black girl. My call went viral! Instead of twelve letters, I got more than fifty from all over the world. And I continue to receive them. On scented paper. Through the internet. Shoved into my hands in Starbucks. Neatly printed on notebook paper. Typed. Scrawled in elegant swirls. In hand-decorated envelopes. Packaged in passed envelopes between a stack of journals.

Hardly anybody sends letters anymore. (Have you even ever written one?) There is something about a letter that demands thoughtfulness and care. You must choose the right paper. You must find the right words. You need a stamp and maybe a trip to the post office. A letter requires *effort* in an era of quick and easy texts and instant messages. Black women did this. They showed up for Black girls—for *you*. The Letters to Black Girls Project was born.

I still get letters from Black women and pass them to Black girls. I wish you could read them all. There is so much love and truth in them that sometimes it makes me cry. But I cannot get every letter to every Black girl, so I wrote this book—*Dear Black Girl: Letters from Your Sisters on Stepping into Your Power*.

Here you will find some of the best letters written by Black women to Black girls and young women about experiences we share, like feeling depressed or battling unfair rules or feeling unsure about our identities. But first, in the introduction, I will explain both where those fixed, negative ideas about us came from and why they are so hard to shake. At the end of each chapter, I invite you to write "Letter(s) to My Black Girl Self." This is important. The most valuable thing you can learn from this book is to be honest and loving with yourself. Do that and you will find it easier to be supportive of other Black girls and women. Also tucked throughout the book are sections titled "Know This." These are bits of information that may help you understand the chapter you just read more clearly or introduce you to awesome Black women and girls and moments in Black history you may want to get to know better.

This book is an antidote to the world's ugly, unforgiving gaze—a balm for the wounds of anti–Black girlness. It is for you. I hope it feels that way. Even if you are really no longer a girl, but a woman. There is wisdom here that we all can use. And even if many people challenge your right to call yourself a girl. To my trans sisters: Welcome. I see you. I love you. Thank you for being here.

Read this book from start to finish or use the index to find just the right letter for what you are facing or feeling at any given moment. Share a letter with your bestie when she needs it. Read them along with your mom, your grandmother, your auntie, or another Black woman to start an important honest conversation.

In this book, Black women will set aside our fears and our hurt to model the way we need to love and care for each other. We will approach you with love, honesty, vulnerability, and grace. Because you are us. We are you. We are alright. And we love you.

— *Know This* —

EUROPEAN BEAUTY STANDARDS are how American society evaluates attractiveness, preferring features commonly associated with white people, such as fine, straight hair; light skin and eyes; and narrow, high-bridged noses. These standards mean that equally beautiful kinky hair; brown skin; dark eyes; and broad, flatter noses are not complimented or praised as they should be.

FEMININITY refers to qualities traditionally associated with women or girls, such as prettiness, quietness, and sweetness, or love for dresses, makeup, and boys. But it is important to remember that women and girls have a wide range of attributes. Embrace yours, whether they are traditionally feminine, masculine, or otherwise.

HYPERSEXUAL refers to an excessive interest in sex.

INTERNALIZED OPPRESSION happens when oppressed people start to believe the lies that oppressors tell about them, including that they are inferior. An example would be a Black woman thinking that Black girls are too "mannish," that they are too loud or "fast," and that they need coaching to be more "ladylike."

LGBTQ+ stands for lesbian, gay, bisexual, transgender, queer/questioning, plus intersex, asexual, non-binary, and other identities.

PUSHOUT SCHOOLS have rules and punishments that take students out of class and sometimes out of school, depriving them of a chance to learn. Students of color, students with disabilities, and LGBTQ+ students are more likely to be pushed out of school.

RESPECTABILITY POLITICS are the belief that by conforming to mainstream (white, straight, middle class, Christian) customs, values, beliefs, and behaviors, Black girls and other oppressed people can avoid prejudice. For example, believing that if a young Black woman takes out her braids and loses her "Blaccent," she can avoid discrimination at her job and excel, or that if a young Black man stops sagging his pants and cuts his locs, he will not be harassed by police.

STREET HARASSMENT occurs when someone forces unwanted sexual attention, comments, gestures, and actions on a stranger in a public place without consent, according to *StopStreetHarassment.org*. For instance, if someone follows you, demanding that you speak to them or provide your name and number, that is street harassment.

TRAUMA refers to bad experiences—abuse, witnessing violence, losing a family member, having parents who divorce, or something else—that stay with you and cause fear, sadness, worry, and insecurity.

INTRODUCTION

You a Lie and the Truth Ain't in Ya

Black girl, I hope you like history. I'm about to give you a little of it. Wait! Don't skip this part. It's important. I need you to know the roots of some of the unfair and untrue things you hear about Black girls—why sometimes people don't treat us right.

Hundreds of years ago, Europeans colonized America using the forced free labor of enslaved African people, including many women and girls—our ancestors. They bought and sold our foremothers, worked them in fields and shops, used them for sex, bred them in order to enslave their sons and daughters, and sometimes sold those children while making our great-great-grandmothers care for the white children of their masters. To justify this horrible treatment, society began to spread the lie that Black women and girls were less human. This is where the fixed, negative beliefs about us come from.

They said that Black women and girls were physically tough, so it did not matter if they worked hard in the hot Southern sun from sunup to sundown. It did not matter if they were punished harshly for minor mistakes or nothing at all. They said Black women were sexually out of control, so it did not matter if they had to stand naked in a market, waiting to be sold, or that they were bred like pit bulls, or that many were repeatedly raped. And to make extra sure that this sexual assault was not seen as a violation by white men, they said Black women and girls were ugly and unwanted, especially compared to prized white women and girls. They said Black women and girls did not have human, loving feelings, so they would not miss their loved ones when they were sold away; they would not be anxious or sad. They said Black women and girls did not have their own needs or wishes, so it cost them nothing to spend all their time and energy taking care of other people. They said Black women and girls were not "ladylike" as white women and girls were, so it did not matter that while those women were protected and placed on pedestals, Black women and girls were treated like beasts. They said Black girls were barely human children at all, so it didn't matter if they were forced to see and do grown folks' things.

Those bad and dehumanizing beliefs still stick to Black women, and I have spent many years writing about the way that they do. A few years ago, I wrote a book called *The Sisters Are Alright: Changing the Broken Narrative of Black Women in America*. I interviewed about one hundred Black women from across the country about how stereotypes affect their lives today and how they have managed to be alright despite it. But I didn't fully understand how early we are forced to deal with this sexism and racism until I spent more time listening to Black girls and learning about *your* experiences.

My girl DeShong and I have been capturing Black girl voices for another book project that we hope will guide adults to support Black girls better. We've conducted one-on-one and group interviews, plus photovoice projects, where you have told us things through photographs. We also have spent time with you on your turf—in classrooms, homes, and other places—to see what you do and say when most adults are not watching.

We were happy to discover that you know our "Black magic" is real and amazing and that you have lots of Black girl role models: from actresses like Marsai Martin and Yara Shahidi to activists like Marley Dias, who created a library of Black girl books, and Naomi Wadler, who gave a powerful speech to thousands at the 2018 Women's March.

But we also learned that even if you cannot quite explain why, you sometimes feel like Ciara, then a high school junior in Pittsburgh. "Everybody hates us," she said. You sense, even if you cannot articulate it, that you are on the end of the broken gaze I wrote about in the preface to this book. And you are not wrong. Those old disgusting beliefs, created centuries ago to enslave Black girls, are still working today.

They say that Black girls are physically tough, so it does not matter if you are treated roughly, like in the viral 2015 video that showed a school resource officer flipping a Black teenage girl named Shakara backward from her chair, dragging her to the front of the room, and handcuffing her for refusing to put away her phone. Or in the other video that circulated around the web that year that showed a police officer, called to break up a pool party in Texas, sitting on top of Dajerria Becton, a tiny Black girl in a swimsuit, and violently restraining her. People often ignore violence against Black girls—even when it comes from people who should love them best, like parents or boyfriends. Even Black girls sometimes ignore the violence. I will never forget that one Black girl we interviewed said we could call her "Mrs. Chris Brown"—even though the singer has admitted to beating one ex-girlfriend and another reportedly has a five-year restraining order against him.

It does not seem to matter if Black girls are punished harshly for minor mistakes or nothing at all. Black girls are more likely to be suspended from school (even though you don't misbehave any more than other girls). You are suspended from school at a rate six times higher than white girls.[1] And you are the fastest growing segment of the juvenile justice system, 1.2 times more likely to be detained and 20 percent more likely to be charged than your white friends.[2]

They say Black girls are sexually out of control, so it does not matter that Black girl bodies are often automatically read as sexual. 40 to 60 percent of Black girls report experiencing sexual assault—unwanted sex or touching—before they are eighteen.[3] And when those girls report their assaults, they are less likely to be believed. Black girls are more likely to be given school dress code violations, and schools with more Black girls have more and stricter rules of dress.[4] One principal on the South Side of Chicago claimed she could stop sexual assault by preventing her mostly Black girl students from dressing "provocatively," instead of teaching boys the importance of consent. Black girls are more likely than other girls to be victims of sex trafficking, according to Grantmakers for Girls of Color.[5] And Black radio still bumps R. Kelly, and the NAACP gave the "Ignition" singer an Image Award, despite numerous Black girls describing how he preyed on them in and outside of schools in Chicago. And how often have you heard Black women and girls called THOTs and hoes?

They say Black girls are ugly and unwanted, especially compared to "prized" white women and girls. When my friend and I speak to Black girls in mostly white, suburban schools, they often tell us how boys—even the Black ones—seek out white girls to date, while ignoring Black girls and branding them "ghetto." Folks—even famous ones—feel comfortable publicly demeaning Black girls' looks and value without fear. A few years ago, the rapper Kodak Black went on Instagram Live to tell his over three million followers, "I don't really like Black girls like that," while naming Kylie Jenner, Ariana Grande, and Miley Cyrus as the objects of his #WomanCrushWednesday. The dark-skinned "No Flockin" performer said women with his same complexion were "too gutter . . . my complexion . . . we too gutter. Light-skinned women—they more sensitive."[6] You see, they *still* say Black women and girls are not as "ladylike" as white women and girls, so it does not matter that while those women are protected and placed on pedestals, Black women and girls are treated like beasts.

They say Black girls do not have human, loving feelings, so they will not miss the people they love when they go away. Many Black girls are separated from parents or other loved ones who are in jail or prison. Too many have lost family, friends, neighbors, and classmates to violence. And those girls are often expected to deal with those separations and losses like the adults around them do—without professional help. Because they say Black girls cannot be anxious or sad—even when faced with all that unfair treatment and disregard and violence, even though sometimes human brains are weird and need help to do right. People think Black girls are tough, strong—descended from women who can watch their babies sold away—they don't need therapy or meds. But a 2009 African American Policy Forum report revealed that 67 percent of Black girls said that they have felt sad or hopeless for two or more weeks straight.[7]

They say Black girls do not have their own needs or wishes, so it costs them nothing to spend all their time and energy taking care of other people. They say Black girls are barely human children at all, so it doesn't matter if they are forced to see and do grown folks' things. A 2017 study by the Georgetown Law Center on Poverty and Inequality found that adults—no matter what race they are or how smart they are—tend to believe Black girls are "less innocent and more adult-like than their white peers, especially in the age range of 5–14."[8] (Five!) They think Black girls need less nurturing, protection, support, and comfort and see Black girls as more independent and knowledgeable about adult topics.

Breathe.

And remember that these are lies.

I know. When you hear a lie so often, it's hard to remember that it isn't true, even when you know better.

Has your grandmother ever turned up her nose at your "nappy," "undone" hair? Have you clowned another Black girl for her dark skin? Do you hide your natural hair texture, because straighter hair, softer hair, or looser curls are just, somehow, prettier to you? Has your mama called you "fast"? Have you believed that a Black girl victim of assault must have done something to deserve it? Do you still check for male superstars who treat Black girls badly? Has a Black woman school counselor suggested you just get over it when you feel depressed? Are you suffering in silence after losing friends or a parent, because you are a Black girl and Black girls are strong?

See. Even when you are a Black woman or girl who has been hurt by untruths, lies can start to feel like facts. And if Black women and girls have our facts messed up, we can't love ourselves properly. And we sure can't love each other right.

There is this thing some old Black folks used to say to call someone out for telling blatant tales, "You a lie and the truth ain't in ya!" Black women and girls must greet fictions about us with that spirit. We must smother these lies, at last, under Black girl love like the warmth and regard expressed in the pages that follow.

— *Know This* —

COLONIZATION is when a nation settles in and takes control of another land and the people who live there, often erasing history and culture, abusing the native population, and stealing resources. America was colonized by several European countries even though hundreds of Native tribes already lived here. Many countries in Africa were also colonized by Europeans.

MARLEY DIAS is a teen activist and feminist. Tired of reading books about "white boys and dogs," in 2015, she started a drive to collect one thousand books about Black girls. The #1000BlackGirlBooks campaign collected nine thousand books and earned Dias a place on the *Forbes* "30 Under 30" list.

ENSLAVE means to take away someone's freedom. Your ancestors were not "slaves"; they were African men and women who were "enslaved" by colonizers.

MARSAI MARTIN is the young actress who plays Diane on *Black-ish*. She has appeared on other TV shows and in films, including 2019's *Little*. In June 2020, she clapped back at internet trolls who criticized her appearance on the annual

BET Awards. Some people complained that the fifteen-year-old was styled to look too old. Martin cautioned, "Let me live!"

SEX TRAFFICKING is what happens when someone is forced or tricked into performing sex acts for money.

YARA SHAHIDI is the young actress who plays Zoey on *Black-ish* and its spin-off *Grown-ish*. She has appeared on other TV shows and in films, including *The Sun Is Also a Star*. She is also an activist who speaks up on a variety of issues important to her. Shahidi, who will attend Harvard University, received a college recommendation from Forever First Black Girl, Michelle Obama.

NAOMI WADLER is a young activist who famously spoke against gun violence at the 2018 March for Our Lives in Washington, DC, when she was just twelve years old.

CHAPTER 1

BLACK GIRL MAGIC

Identity and Self-Love

I SEE YOU SPARKLING

In my book *The Sisters Are Alright: Changing the Broken Narrative of Black Women in America*, I wrote that there is nothing wrong with Black women (or girls). "We have facets like diamonds. The trouble is the people who refuse to see us sparkling."[1]

A woman named CaShawn Thompson put a name to the way Black girls shine. In 2013, she tweeted, "Black girls are magic. You can do anything." That tweet became the hashtag #Black-GirlMagic. On *blkhistoryuntold.com*, CaShawn said, "I always thought that we were magic. I thought that maybe I wasn't yet but look at Mommy and look at Grandma and look at Auntie. 'I'll grow older; I'll be magic, too.' But what I understood to be magic was fairytales, witches and people that could work spells and make things out of no things and make things happen that nobody else could, and that's what I saw [in Black women]."[2]

Now you see the term "Black girl magic" everywhere. T-shirts. Books. Workshops. What you don't see is CaShawn's name. "I wasn't the right kind of woman to be saying these things . . . I wasn't the college grad . . . I didn't have the money . . . I was older . . . when I did this I was poor, divorced, a single mother . . . A lot of it had to do with who thought I was worthy of the credit," she told For Harriet, a website for Black women.[3] Those fixed, negative ideas about us didn't stop CaShawn's genius, but they blocked her brilliance from public view.

You may know that feeling. Sometimes it seems like Black girls have to be perfect for people to love them. A little sister has to be born in the right zip code. She has to have the right sort of family. She has to look the right way—the right skin tone, right curves, contour in the right places. She has to be agreeable, no matter what she endures. She must never be tired or fed up or loud or angry or sad. She must like boys and only boys, but not like them too much. She must be ladylike. Innocent but grown up. She can't just be human. She can't just be worthy because of that. Sometimes it's hard to remember that you are a star when the world doesn't reflect your light. But you *are* a star—a bright one.

In the letters that follow, Black women recognize your shine, and they tell you what to remember to stay gleaming and strong in your Black girlhood—how they keep the magic when folks challenge their beauty or smarts or who they love or their right to just *be*. Here are the spells, Black girl. Use your magic to make the haters disappear. Poof!

Sparkle on.

....

DEAR ONE,

Where is your light?

What is the one, shining thing that makes you yourself?

Is it the way you walk?

The way you talk?

Is it the way your lip curls when you smile?

Do you have a mole on your cheekbone?

Does your hair wind around a certain way when it's wet?

Do you blush when you are embarrassed?

Is your skin tone hot butter browning in a pan or dark chocolate?

Are you loud and boisterous?

Are you reserved and shy?

Can you sit by yourself without getting lonely?

Are you most comfortable in a crowd?

Do you believe in justice?

Do you believe in God?

Does music make you soar?

I ask these things, because I urge you to know.

Know your light. Know where it resides.

That is the key to everything.

A dictionary defines light as *the natural agent that stimulates sight and makes things visible.* When you begin to see your own light—that special thing that makes you like no other, guard it. Do not let anyone steal or dim your light.

There are times when you won't feel so special, and your light won't feel so bright; there are times when you don't want to shine, and you will pray that no one notices you—you just want to fade into the beige background and hide your light from everyone, so they won't see you.

I know this, because I have felt those things, too. There were times when I was feeling sorry for myself and my mother would say, "Stop crying. Wipe those tears." And I would cry louder and longer, because I was angry at her for not joining me in feeling sorry for myself—joining my "pity party."

Eleanor Roosevelt was a very wise First Lady. Her husband was President Franklin Roosevelt. She once said that "No one can make you feel inferior without your consent."

There will be times when it will seem like the world is conspiring against you in an effort to make you feel less-than. You are not skinny enough. Your hair isn't straight enough or long enough. You don't have the latest clothes or the best designer shoes. That one over there is smarter/prettier/skinnier/more popular than you.

Sometimes you want to react with anger at people who you think are "making" you feel a certain way. But remember what Mrs. Eleanor said: "No one can make you feel inferior without your consent."

It's on you. You are the only one in charge of your light. Remember that. No one can dim it without your permission. You have the igniter. And you must guard it with your whole being.

If you ever, ever think that extinguishing your light forever is the answer, seek help. Find a stronger light to help you keep yours going. You are one of many who light the world. Whether you think so or not, the planet will be diminished without you. And when others—mothers, mentors, aunties—help you keep your light going, pass it on. Help someone else. You will see yourself reflected in them.

I ask you to remember that your mother was once a girl. So was your grandmother, and her mother, and her mother before her. Those women each had their own light, just like you have your own. They each had their own igniter, and they each met some of the same challenges you are facing and will face in the future.

I can tell you they made many mistakes. They fear you will make the same ones. You probably will make mistakes. Wherever there is light, there is shadow.

These women hope you will learn from them just as they did (or didn't) from other women, and that you will not repeat mistakes without learning the valuable lessons that follow; that you will use your own light to guide your way and will be a source of light for others.

A wise woman whose opinions I revere greatly, Marian Wright Edelman, once wrote a book in which she addressed her sons. "Sell the shadow for the substance," she counseled them. "Don't confuse style with meaning. Get your insides in order and your direction clear first and then worry about your clothes and your wheels."[4]

Sell the shadow. Use your light to shine for justice.

There is a song that Civil Rights workers sang, "This Little Light of Mine." Their clarion voices rang out in the face of terrible injustices and long odds. There are many things wrong in the world. When you see injustice, don't turn your light inward.

Your light is your superpower. Hold it high for all to behold.

Let it shine.

Let it shine.

Let it shine.

With Love, your sister in light,

CELESTE

....

DEAR DOPE BLACK GIRL,

You don't know me, but I know you. I know you, because I am you. We are magic, light and stars in the universe! It might not seem like it sometimes because the world tells differently. They say we're "too"— too loud, too quiet, too happy, too angry, too much everything.

Guess what? They're kind of right. We're too amazing for them to ever comprehend. But don't let their fear stop you.

Know that you have millions of sisters behind you and next to you. And we love you exactly as you are.

Keep being magical, baby sis.

LUMINOUS

Dear Brown-Skinned Black Girl,

If no one else tells you this today, hear it from me: You and your dark chocolate shell, are beautifully and wonderfully made!

As a young girl, growing up with chocolate skin and 4c hair (the tightest of tight kinks and curls), I didn't see anyone on television that looked like me. And if somehow a girl like me did make it to the screen, she was usually being made fun of. That made me feel like I was not beautiful. And I have spent the last 35 years trying to turn that feeling around. I am going to do my best right now to tell you the things I wish someone had told me back then.

Read this as often as you need to be okay.

They hate you because they ain't you. Look around, love, people who don't have what you have and don't look how you look are paying big bucks to get what the Creator bestowed upon you for free. The next time you see a girl on IG, tanned to death, with lip fillers, butt implants and box braids, just remember: Yours is free and organic!

We are slowly—ever so slowly—moving toward a world that sees the beauty in you—in us. As I write this, Miss Universe, Miss America, Miss USA and Miss Teen USA are all beautiful vibrant Black women of varying hues and hair textures. They are a visual representation of all the ways Black girls can be and are physically beautiful.

In the meantime, know that the absence of dark-skinned girls in mainstream culture says more about the people making that culture than it says about you.

As a girl, I remember thinking, "What's wrong with me?" I had a ton of answers and each one made me feel worse than the one before it. I don't want that for you. Bump that!

Your melanin—that thing that controls how brown you are? It is an asset! People may give you crap about it. And you may not appreciate it now. But know this, honey, the saying "Black don't crack" is real and melanin is the best anti-aging cream you could ever ask for.

Beautiful Black girl—If you let it, this world will take your soul and try to convince you that you handed it over willingly. It is my job, as a fellow Black girl, to stop that from happening.

I start by telling you that you are beautiful; the Creator makes no mistakes. But also know that in your beauty lies an ability to do and be anything you want. And if nothing else, know that this chocolate girl loves you.

CAROLYN

(P.S. Hit me up if you ever need to talk. My email is *Carolyn @bulliesslink.com*.)

DEAR BIRACIAL/MULTIRACIAL/MIXED GIRL,

You may be HALF-BLACK/ONE-QUARTER/ONE-EIGHTH/ONE-SIXTEENTH/SOME NEW MATHEMATICAL EQUATION/AN UNKNOWN AMOUNT, but you are not fragmented. You are not EITHER BLACK OR [Any race on or off the census/Any race left blank on your birth certificate]. Though you may be asked over and over, you do not have to choose. You are BLACK AND [Lady's Choice]. If you find yourself simply saying BLACK, you do not need to explain. You do not need to answer the short essay question WHAT ARE YOU? That question is not your problem.

Yes, I recognize your parent. Your DARKER/BIRTH/ADOPTIVE/FOSTER parent. Your LIGHTER/NOT-BLACK/FIRST/ADOPTIVE/FOSTER parent. Even if whitefolks mistake your mom for the nanny. Even if your dad has that accent and that nose. Even if you have two moms or no mom, two dads or no dad. Even if you've NEVER MET/CAN'T SPEAK the language. You belong to your family. Even if your HALF/STEP/ADOPTED/FOSTER/FULL siblings are LIGHTER/NOT-BLACK. Even if your siblings are DARKER/TALLER/SHORTER/SKINNIER/ROUNDER. Even if you're a singleton. Even with that hair of yours.

Blackfolks will accept you. Though probably not now. Not when the only boy who likes you is teased so bad he sends someone to break up with you (even though he's darker than you, his Afro bigger, he's technically MEXICAN/NOT-BLACK). Not when your NOT-BLACK friends confess they think of you as REGULAR/NORMAL/NOT-BLACK. Not the days it feels like you're doing hard time in your SCHOOL/NEIGHBORHOOD/VILLAGE/RESERVATION/COMMUNITY/TOWN/SUBURB/CITY, because there are no other BLACK/BROWN/MIXED kids. Or because there are just enough that you avoid acknowledging each other while anyone's watching. Or because there are so many that the others think you're weird for not knowing HOW TO BE BLACK. Your unfamiliarity with SLANG/ HIPHOP/SORORITIES/CARD-GAMES/DANCE-MOVES/SOUL-FOOD/THE SOUTH doesn't make you any LESS-BLACK. Though for a while, others who, like you, were raised in WHITE FAMILIES/ WHITE SCHOOLS/WHITE SUBURBS will pretend it does. Girls your age can be fearful and mean, but blackwomen will be your greatest allies.

You can be smart. Black Nerds are a thing. Even if your teacher accuses you of plagiarizing, protesting that the paper you spent two weeks writing is far too advanced. Even if the school counselor refuses to recommend you to that fancy, private college, because before he realized that white parent shouting in the office is yours, he said COSMETOLOGY SCHOOL/VO-TECH/COMMUNITY COLLEGE/ THE ARMY was good enough.

You can go to the school dance. Even if you don't have cheerleader looks—white skin and straight blonde hair that can hold a fake curl. Even if you look white but your white mother doesn't know what to do with your hair or how to teach you to love your butt and thighs. Even if you have freckles all over your face instead of velvety chocolate skin like the rest of the family. Even if you don't have that marketable mixed look—golden to olive skin, wild curls and BLUE/GREEN/HAZEL eyes that drive the blackboys wild. Even if you don't like boys and don't want to wear anything that draws attention to your BREASTS/ LACK OF BREASTS. You can go to the school dance, even if there are no AUNTIES/COUSINS/BIG SISTERS to teach you how to move your hips on the dance floor and in the street.

You will figure it out. Even without a strong blackmother, you will learn to flash your palm to check racism before it has a chance to enter you. Even without a strong blackfather, you will learn how to fight your own battles. Even without a blackamerican parent, you will learn that the issue is race, not color, and yes, race certainly matters. But then again, it doesn't define you, because you, well, you are the opportunity for an entire language to change syntax, for entire countries to rewrite census forms and history. You + Are = Enough. You are new math.

FAITH

DEAREST QUEER AND QUESTIONING BLACK GIRL,

There comes a time in life when things start to get interesting and our thoughts shift from schoolwork and television—a time when many of us begin grappling with not only what Blackness means, but also our sexuality and/or our gender presentation. I wish the world we lived in allowed the space for all humans to explore what sexuality means to them. It would be a different world, indeed. As Black and Brown folks living in America, that is not our reality. I know this first-hand because I present to the world as a Black woman. That is something I am proud of. However, I identify as a first-generation, Afro-German non-binary person, as well as a mother, writer, curator and organizer. All of these traits form who I am. I am grateful for every one of them.

I am still learning who I am at the age of 41. I give myself permission to continue learning until my last breath. My journey was not easy and most likely yours will not be either. The journey to self never is. That is what makes life beautiful and worth fighting for. None of our stories are the same. There is no guide to coming out and that's not what this will be. I hope that my words will carry you through the storms and remind you that you are not alone. And the only person that can define you is you. Be patient with yourself. It's not going to be easy, but it will be worth it.

You will go through life hearing horror stories and know the pain of losing people simply for being who you are. Just know that for every one of those stories there are hundreds more queer people in love with their lives. Households filled with people not afraid to love themselves out loud. Streets where you can hold your beloved's hand and be affirmed. Cities that see you for the human you are. You can be successful and gay. You can be trans and accepted. You can be your complete authentic self and find love. You can be gay and proud. AND you can be Black or POC proud.

You create your own narrative. Why not create a space within yourself to be all things? You will find people that will accept you, fully as you are. And the biggest gift you can give yourself is the chance for that future. Your heart will get broken, as does anyone's heart who is brave enough to love. You will have to come out a hundred times and it won't be fair, but it'll be a chance for you to solidify the bond with yourself, as well as let you decide who is worthy of knowing the whole you. Some days the anger will well up inside you and that's okay. Find ways to be angry that don't cause you harm.

Know that just like your Blackness isn't monolithic, you get to decide what being queer looks like for you. There is no need to reduce yourself to a stereotype. Do what makes you happy and comfortable. Take the time you need and don't be ashamed of experimenting. Give yourself the space to find out who you are. Make mistakes but always wear protection. You get to decide how loud you live and on what terms. Do not feel like you have to fit into some mold created by society. Especially a society based off erasure, theft, racism, genocide and bigotry. You come from a long line of people that lived their lives to the fullest and no matter how their lives ended, their stories never did. In those moments of sadness, grief and when you feel like it may just be easier to hide who you are, lean upon our ancestors for the strength to carry on.

This is especially true for those that are in situations where it's dangerous to be out. Hold tight. No matter if you can live authentically today, tomorrow or 20 years from now, you are perfect as you are. Cling to all the stories of survival. If no one, including yourself, has told you today, you are seen. You are loved. You are perfect as you are. Know you are held by ancestors that carried movements and folks on the front lines of revolution today. A lineage of creators that altered the game with every note, word and brush stroke. We are doctors, inventors, CEOs, homemakers, farmers, politicians and more. Bayard Rustin. Josephine Baker. Marsha "Pay It No Mind" Johnson. Sylvia Rivera. Denice Frohman. Janelle Monáe. Little Richard. Frida Kahlo. Tracy Chapman. Deborah Batts. Audre Lorde. James Baldwin. Pauli Murray. You are carried by giants . . . never forget that. You are a gift to this world and no matter what they want you to believe, you are worthy of your own happiness.

TATJANA

....

HEY, BLACK GIRL,

I want to talk to you about your body.

Not in the way that the world talks to you about your body, no. This isn't about your skin color, your hair, or your size. It's not about your "curves" and where they reside on your figure, either.

This is solely about your body and the relationship you develop with it over time. It's about redefining what self-care is and what it can mean for you.

We spend so much time talking about bodies and what they should look like, that we ignore a far more important conversation: what your body has the ability to do.

You are physically capable beyond measure. You can run, jump, climb, lift, build, and, yes, grow with that body. It is yours, and those are your skills to build. And, in the quest to build those skills, you can change the trajectory of your health—both physically and mentally— for the better, in a long term, meaningful way.

People will tell you that being active is about "looking great," or it's about "losing weight," but I want to suggest that you already look good *now*, regardless of whatever size you are. I want you to know that it's okay to love your body as it is in this moment, and I want you to know that there are more reasons to love your body beyond how appealing it is to others.

If you are finally able to get even halfway up that rock climbing wall, and you break down into tears because it's so hard but you really made it halfway and it feels that much more possible now, that's a reason to love your body. It got you somewhere it couldn't before.

If your younger sibling goes flying down the sidewalk towards the intersection on her scooter and you take off running after her to save her, and in the moment you are thankful that you could save her, that's a reason to love your body.

And if you want to love your richly brown skin and your endlessly curly, coily hair, your full figure or your tiny frame, and the twinkle in your brown eye? Of course, you can. You should.

But also know that valuing your body for what it can do gives you a different kind of drive. Skills are meant to be built—train, push yourself, and give yourself the chance to grow. Skills are meant to build character just as much as they're meant to build ability. You are soft and your humanity must always be recognized, but building resilience means you know what it looks and feels like to get back up when you're down. You had to fall off that wall a few times before you even got halfway—getting back up after getting knocked down is a skill set that extends beyond training, too.

Do not let the world tell you the only important thing—or even the most important thing—about your body is what it looks like. It is an essential part of self-care to not only know how to move your body, but know that this movement is the best kind of care for your body.

The most transformative kind of love is the kind that builds you up, helps you feel capable, and gives you the self-esteem to face the world with a clear head, a full heart, and a powerful drive. The kind of self-care that helps you move your body is the truest embodiment of that love that you can give yourself. Embrace it fully, love it deeply, and build it powerfully. You will thrive in the truest sense of the word, and you deserve that, and so much more.

Sincerely,

ERIKA

Hey There, Wonderful Human!

Listen. There will be people who will tell you how to think about what is beautiful and what isn't. They will do this right in your face, knowing that what they describe as beautiful is nothing like the way you look or the way you dress—your beauty, your style.

Friends might talk to you as if you are missing out on something because you prefer to wear more plain clothing or gender nonconforming clothing. Like what old lesbians called androgynous. I want you to know that your style and queer identity is yours to claim and express how you want. *That* is what makes you beautiful—that you find joy living authentically in your skin, loving yourself with flaws and knowing that there will be moments when you are flawless.

Turn off what everyone else has to say in order to quiet yourself and think about what *you* like. Discover what it takes to feel good in your own skin and to feel confidence in what you wear and how you express yourself. It might take some time and trials to figure it out. Claim it. Once you do, challenge yourself to express it. You can do it. Know that you can choose to not conform to what Black girls and young women, yes even queer ones, are "supposed" to look like. I understand that fitting in is sometimes important, but if fitting in means that you have to leave some of who you are and how you want to express yourself behind, then take time to think it through. Ask yourself if it's worth it. You get to decide. I'm rooting for you. I want you to thrive and know that you are a beautiful human being.

Sincerely,

Seven

....

DEAR BLACK GIRL!

Whatever is growing out of your head is beautiful.

Do not let them tell you different.

In this day and age, where folks are constantly making YouTube videos about "the big chop" and "why I went natural," a part of me wants to laugh. When I went "natural" more than 25 years ago before, it was considered abnormal. Not something you *want* to do. In my conservative corner of the Midwest even among other Black people I was criticized and shunned for my hair.

Once while I was growing out my TWA (teeny-weeny afro), I was out at the grocery with an older family member. They were so ashamed of my hair, they refused to introduce me to their co-worker. I was hurt, but not stunned. That moment gave me more strength to know I was headed in the right direction for me. But let's back track a bit.

At the time I chopped, I was 19 years old and a sophomore in college. I was suffering a serious identity crisis, which ultimately plunged me into a deep well of depression. Thanks to a strong support network, I was able to climb out of confusion and feelings of worthlessness and despair. While pulling towards a different life, I looked in the mirror one day and realized that the hair on top of my head just didn't make sense. I did not understand something so basic about myself as this stuff growing out of my body. As I fought to regain a sense of self and love of self, I had to learn to love *all* the pieces of myself including every single kinky strand growing on my head.

On a spring day in 1993, I woke up, called the barber, sat down in that chair, and asked them to shave my head. The barber was confused. My hair hung past my shoulders at the time. "All of it?" He asked. "All of it," I said. That confused him. He convinced me to get a "texturizer" after cutting my hair down to one inch. I didn't realize at the time that "texturizer" is code for a relaxer taken out quickly, so the hair doesn't completely straighten. I hated my "texturized" hair even more than the straightened hair, as it looked like a bad attempt at trying to be something that I was not. I needed to be me in the raw.

A month later, I went to a different barber and had him shave my head bald. I will spare you all the details, but the early part of my natural hair journey was intense and often lonely. Back then, most Black haircare products were made for straightened hair and those messed with my tresses. It was years of trial by fire, experimenting with everything on the shelf and new hairstyles that hadn't become mainstream yet—twists, Bantu knots, cornrow styles and more. But most often for a long time, I went straight old school with Blue Magic or Royal Crown hair grease, a stiff brush, water and occasionally a pressing comb. I wore extension hair braids for years, not realizing the chemicals in that plastic hair were damaging my hair. The more I learned, the more I became comfortable with my hair and six years after the first chop, I got chopped again to remove all the hair damaged by pressing comb straightening and never-ending braiding. That second chop has been with me for nearly 17 years now.

I tell this story not because I am encouraging you to cut your hair or even because I think this outdated journey will make sense to you today. I tell you this story because there will be times in your life when you must reach within and find yourself. When you must learn to let go of people's notions about you and what you should be. And when you do this, you may find you walk alone—that your journey and strength to follow the beat of your own drum is the encouragement others need to find themselves and be set free.

This lesson about hair is applied to all of life. For the rest of your life. Be brave my queen. You are descended from powerful people.

You have what it takes.

You are beautiful.

As is.

You are enough.

Namaskar!

EVETTE

To a Magical Black Girl,

First things first: I want you to know what an honor and a privilege it is for me to be able to write to you. I've been thinking a great deal lately about the kinds of things I would have wanted to hear from a Black woman when I was growing up and figuring *myself* out. I hope what I have to say will be helpful to you. These things are important for me to say and, I think, important for you to hear.

Growing up I was a very passionate reader. I especially loved fairy tales, folk tales, and fantasy novels—stories where a kid stumbled across some magical object, book or hidden power that took them on exciting adventures. When I was much older, I realized that I had to make some mental adjustments to relate to these stories. The kids in them never looked anything like me. The main characters were usually boys, with girls in the background. And heroes were always white. Sometimes I would mentally insert myself into the story, because I didn't see why a young brown-skinned girl couldn't be magical or powerful or be the one who saves the day. I don't want you to have to do that. I want you to have new stories, new adventures, and new dreams, without having to change anything to make room for you. I want you to know that "Black girl magic" means something. It is not just a way to sell tote bags or sparkly eye shadow.

My beloved fantasy stories were a way to hold on to a childhood that I felt was slipping away, or more accurately, being taken away. I was a bookish and smart little girl and people often treated me as if I understood things or could make decisions far beyond my years. My body grew and developed early, and some adults behaved toward me as if I were an adult too. There were many times that men said inappropriate things to me or made me feel uncomfortable. The people

I should have been able to confide in—the adults who should have protected me—sometimes seemed to blame me for the bad behavior of others.

I was a good student, but sometimes teachers seemed doubtful that my work was my own. And why did I feel that adults in my life were disappointed that I wasn't interested in things they thought I should be good at, like sports, and suspicious of the things I *was* good at, like writing or acting? I learned not to show my anger or fear or even sadness, because those emotions seemed to be off-limits to me; I was punished or criticized for showing them. My white friends could throw tantrums, talk back, be defiant in class, and make mistakes without being treated as if they had committed a terrible crime. But I learned to be still, quiet, strong, and always stay in control. It was a survival technique, and I still see too many young Black girls being forced to do the same. Black girls and women are not allowed to display our full range of emotions, to be *too* smart, or to need help. We are not given the space to figure things out for ourselves.

Do these things sound familiar? They are common to the experiences of Black girls. If what I have shared does not mirror your experiences, it probably connects to someone you know. If this letter does anything, I hope it makes clear that women like me, who were once Black girls like you, are out here. We see you. Your voice matters and we're listening.

My favorite stories also helped me feel okay about wanting to explore and express myself. Maybe, most importantly, they helped me see myself as a complicated, whole person. I learned to use my own creativity and imagination to push boundaries and create a place for myself in a world that sometimes didn't seem to know what to do with me. First books did this for me; later it was movies, TV shows, and performances in plays and speech tournaments. For you, something different—basketball, cooking, doing hair or makeup, or something else may give you hope.

I have hopes for you.

I hope you truly get to be a kid, and to have fun, to play games, to be innocent, to feel joy, and to feel free.

I hope part of that freedom is to explore, to push boundaries, to mess up, and to get the chance to learn and grow from it when you do.

I hope you discover your own strength and power and aren't afraid to use it.

I also hope you find out that it's ok to not feel strong all the time; that it's healthy and normal to sometimes feel vulnerable, and to need comfort and protection. And that you *deserve* to have it.

I hope you know that you have a right to anger, and that you shouldn't be shamed or punished for expressing that anger in healthy ways.

I hope that every aspect of your life will nurture your love, particularly your self-love. I hope you appreciate the beauty of you, from the color of your skin to the way your hair grows, to the body that supports and moves you through the world.

I hope you know that you have the right to feel safe and set boundaries around that body. It belongs to you and you are the one who gets to make decisions about it. I hope there is someone knowledgeable and experienced who you trust if you need help making those decisions.

I hope you know that you are a person of incredible potential and untold capabilities, and the world is open to you in ways you may not be able to imagine now. If something interests or motivates you, I hope you pursue it, even if the path seems difficult or unsure.

I hope you learn to use your voice to express yourself, advocate for yourself or others, and to use it to cry, scream, laugh, sing, yell or do whatever you need to do to feel heard.

And I hope you find stories you love that inspire you to create your own very potent form of Black girl magic. Your own magic is better than the spells in any fairy tale or fantasy movie. And it is yours entirely.

Wishing you the very best of everything,

ADRIANNE

....

My Trans Sisters,

To be a young, trans person of color is nothing to be ashamed or afraid of. On the contrary, you should celebrate with joy, love and pride. If only I could have been brave, bold and true when I was your age!

My transition and acceptance came later in life. I didn't come out until I was 26 years old. I always knew who I was. In my earliest memories I recall knowing that I was meant to be one of the girls. Being one of the boys just didn't make any sense.

Since I didn't start my transition until I was 26, I spent my entire teen years and early 20s never, ever feeling comfortable, sexy or powerful in my own skin. I just felt lost and misplaced.

When I started my transition and my hair got longer, I remember the ecstatic feeling of seeing these tight, kinky coils of curly hair growing out. They had laid dormant for far too long. I started to play around with it in several different styles. I still remember how amazingly beautiful I felt seeing myself in the mirror with my Afro, bra and panties on. It was an image I had often admired and yearned for. It was finally me! I felt powerful, confident, sexy—like a goddess!

I couldn't believe it took me all these years, but it finally happened. That is why I am so proud of you for being you. Being transgender is not a curse; it is a gift—a liberating gift. You have the power to authentically live your life and present the way you have always felt is right. When you are emotionally aligned with your physical self, nothing in the world can stop you.

Family and friends may not have been as supportive as you hoped when you came out. Know that they are dealing with a lot of things also—just as you did before coming to your resolve to transition. It's hard coming out as trans. It is different than coming out as gay or lesbian. You are coming out to the world as a different being entirely.

Family and friends will always have mixed reactions and feelings. It took me several years to understand that some family and friends are grieving the loss of who they once knew and the gender they once identified with me. Essentially my pre-transition self is dead. Gone forever. Some family and friends need time to grieve that loss. Some never recover and never accept; others will. That doesn't make any lack of support justified. Maybe it offers some perspective. People who really love and care for you will come back around.

It can be a scary thing to be a trans person of color. We see in the media all the time how trans women of color are attacked and murdered. This can be enough to make anyone want to hide and not live their true lives. But that is not who we are. That is not what we do. We have suffered too much to hide in the dark. Life is meant to be lived open and free. That's what we will do together. Our community of trans brothers and sisters is strong. You'll never be alone. There is always someone that has your back.

Stay true to your head and heart. The world is yours.

Love,

BAILEY

— *Know This* —

JOSEPHINE BAKER was an American-born dancer who, refusing to perform for segregated audiences in the United States, made her fame in Paris, France. She served in the French Resistance during World War II and was active in the civil rights movement.

JAMES BALDWIN was an American novelist, playwright, essayist, poet, and activist. He was the author of important literary works, including *The Fire Next Time* and *Notes of a Native Son*.

THE HONORABLE DEBORAH BATTS was a United States district judge who served the borough of Manhattan. She was the first openly gay Black federal judge.

THE BIG CHOP happens when Black women or girls cut off all their processed hair to reveal only their naturally textured hair. The Big Chop sometimes results in a TWA (Teeny Weeny Afro).

"BLACK DON'T CRACK" is a common saying in the Black community. The darker your skin the more melanin you have, meaning protection from sun damage and wrinkles. Darker skin can age more slowly, making Black women appear ageless.

TRACY CHAPMAN is a singer/songwriter known best for her 1988 hit "Fast Car."

MARIAN WRIGHT EDELMAN is a children's rights activist and the founder of the Children's Defense Fund.

DENICE FROHMAN is a poet, writer, performer, and educator who explores race, gender, and sexuality.

MARSHA P. JOHNSON was an activist, self-identified drag queen, performer, and survivor. She was a prominent figure in the Stonewall uprising of 1969. The "P" stood for "Pay It No Mind," which is what Marsha would say in response to questions about her gender.

FRIDA KAHLO was a famed Mexican painter known especially for her self-portraits. Her work explored race, class, and gender in Mexican society.

LITTLE RICHARD, whose real name was Richard Penniman, was a singer, songwriter, and musician. Known as "the Architect of Rock and Roll," he influenced some of music's greatest acts.

AUDRE LORDE was a writer, feminist, and activist who described herself as a "Black, lesbian, mother, warrior poet." She is known for works including the book *Sister Outsider: Essays and Speeches*.

JANELLE MONÁE is a singer and actress known for her albums *The Electric Lady* and *Dirty Computer* and roles in films including *Hidden Figures*.

PAULI MURRAY was an Episcopal priest, attorney, and civil rights activist who worked to end discrimination against women and people of color.

NAMASKAR is a Sanskrit word that translates to "I bow toward your existence."

NON-BINARY or genderqueer refers to an identity that is neither exclusively male nor female.

Letter writer Tatjana says **QUEER** "is the term I use for LGBTQIA+ folks. It is used with the deepest of love and admiration. I use this term as a means of full inclusion to represent all folks across the vast spectrum that is sexuality and gender presentation."

SYLVIA RIVERA was a gay and transgender rights activist.

ELEANOR ROOSEVELT was the wife of President Franklin Delano Roosevelt and served as First Lady of the United States from 1933 to 1945. She was also a diplomat and activist who worked on behalf of civil rights for Black people and women.

BAYARD RUSTIN, who worked closely with Dr. Martin Luther King Jr., was a key figure in several social movements, including fights against the oppression of people of color and gay people. He is credited with teaching Dr. King about nonviolence and with helping to plan the March on Washington for Jobs and Freedom in 1963.

CASHAWN THOMPSON is the originator of the term "Black girl magic."

Letter to My Black Girl Self

Black girl, where does your magic lie? Write a letter about the things you love about your Black girl self. Think about you in your fullness—your Blackness, your girlhood, and the other identities you may have. Remind yourself why and how you shine!

CHAPTER 2

IT (FOR REAL) TAKES A VILLAGE

Family Relationships

WHO YOUR PEOPLE?

"Who your people?"

Maybe you've heard that question before—from an elder at your church or a friend of the family. Ms. Washington peers over her glasses and leans heavy on her cane, feathers of her Sunday hat tickling your face, and asks, "Who your people?"

What she means is, Who do you belong to? Who is guiding you? Whose rituals and customs will you carry on? Who holds you and holds you down? Who makes you feel safe? Who takes care of you? Who supports your dreams? Who do you laugh with? Who do you love? Who loves you? Who is your family?

Everybody gotta have people. People are important. Family is important.

For some Black girls, family looks like a married mom and dad loving each other and loving their girl with lots of support from grandparents and aunties and uncles and ancestors and friends. My people are like this. We are connected by blood. My parents have been married for more than fifty years! I love them. Society praises families like mine—"traditional" families. And my people *are* pretty great. But most Black girls' people don't look exactly like this. That doesn't mean you don't have family.

Family—your people—can take many forms. You can have a big mama and a bunch of uncles who love you. You can have a mommy at home and a daddy loving you from across town. You can have a dad and a papa or two mamas. You can have a divorced mom and dad and a bonus mom. You can have a loving foster family. Your parents may have chosen you specially, and that choice makes you theirs and they are yours and there is no blood involved. Your friends can be your chosen family.

Family is more than blood. Black folks know this. We've always had "play cousins" and second mamas and neighborhood aunties. Don't let your ideas about family be narrow, fixed, and negative. Our people's understanding of family is as broad and wide as the Atlantic Ocean. It's an understanding that is "in our blood." Several African cultures have proverbs that translate to "It takes a village to raise a child."

In Uganda, they say, *Omwana takulila nju emoi*. A child does not grow up only in a single home.

The Bantu people say, *Omwana taba womoi*. A child belongs not to one parent or home.

The Wajita people say, *Omwana ni wa bhone.* Regardless of a child's biological parents, its upbringing belongs to the community.

In Swahili, *Asiye funzwa na mamae hufunzwa na ulimwengu.* Whomsoever is not taught by the mother will be taught with the world.

You, Black girl, have people. Be they many or a few, related by blood or love, they are valid.

One more thing, girl. Now, folks like to keep this on the low—sometimes your people can be difficult. Sometimes your family doesn't love you perfectly, because they are human and that makes them imperfect. Sometimes—a lot of the time—people ain't easy. Sometimes you have to learn to accept your people's flaws to love them and let them love you. Sometimes your family cannot accept you as your full self and they reject you. Too many queer Black girls know this reality. Sometimes you realize that some of your people don't deserve to be your people anymore.

In the letters that follow, Black women write to you about the fabulous but messy reality of family.

....

Dear Young Queens Raised by People Who Aren't Your Mothers and Fathers,

I want to tell you something that someone else might not until after you have experienced years of sadness, feeling different or out of step, or wishing for something, or someone, you don't have.

I want to help lift that sadness. I want to offer you a look at a family that may look more like yours.

But first, I need to tell you something that is true: There is no single definition of family.

There are traditional families made up of a father, mother and 2.5 children (which makes no sense because no one has half a child).

There are single-parent families who are constantly branded less-than other families.

But to try to brand every family with a single label is wrong. Every family filled with love is right.

So, this letter, these words of love, dear hearts, are for those of you like me, members of "made families." Like the ones where Big Mama runs the house, but she's not really your mom, and your dad is not your dad, but is an uncle or grandfather or family friend.

Let me tell you about my made family.

When I was 3 years old, I was growing up with my brother in a New York City apartment. Soon after my sister's birth, my mother contracted multiple sclerosis, my parents broke up, and my maternal grandmother, the only one I ever knew, charged into Grand Central Terminal like a Confederate general retrieving a lost heritage. She bundled up my mother, my siblings and me and packed us up for a lonely Amtrak train ride, a sad journey from the grand, gritty spirit of New York to a slower-paced, Southern-to-a-fault small town in North Carolina.

I spent the next 15 years missing my father, and wishing for a conventional family with a father, mother and children. I prayed for him to show up on a white horse, gather us all up and take us back to the Big Apple.

Every year, I wished for him. Every year, he didn't come. I also lived with the guilt of wanting him, while my grandparents made sure they provided everything I would need to become the best me possible: a good education, every opportunity I asked for every year and more love than I ever deserved.

My grandfather worked three jobs to make ends meet. My grandmother was a homemaker who also helped care for any other children who needed her. My grandparents became my parents.

When I wanted to join the high school band, they bought me a clarinet.

When I made the cheerleading squad, they bought the uniform.

When I was accepted early into the University of North Carolina at Chapel Hill, they made sure I could go.

I remember the day my grandfather, dressed in his best Sunday suit, drove us west to my future. He was so proud. My grandmother was so proud.

And there I was, all of 18 years old, finally realizing that the father I had yearned for all those years wasn't coming back—and the father who made sure I had everything I ever needed was sitting in the driver's seat and loved me most of all.

And the mother I felt I had lost because she had lost the use of her limbs still cheered me on while my grandmother became the mother who nursed emotional and physical wounds, taught me how to make coffee and used to let me sit on the floor, my head on her knee while she scratched my scalp.

And when I entered my junior year and needed an internship to prove that my journalism skills could be used in the real world, I didn't look for or even think about my father.

I earned the internship. But the newspaper, *The News & Observer*, was in Raleigh, N.C., the state capitol, about 40 minutes from Chapel Hill by car.

And I didn't have a car.

So, the weekend after I got the good news, I climbed aboard a Greyhound bus, the mode of transport I'd used for two years to go home from college. Defeated, deflated and bereft of hope, I got to the house and threw myself into bed.

Suddenly, my grandfather knocked on my bedroom door.

"What's wrong with you?" he asked gruffly. He was a gruff man. Loving but gruff.

I told him that I'd gotten a job at a newspaper, but the newspaper was too far away from campus for me to accept it. I told him that I'd just wasted two years, and I would never write an article that could help me get a full-time job. I told him I may as well stay home and work at the gas station downtown that was owned by a high school classmate's father.

He didn't speak again.

But the next morning, early Saturday, he knocked on my door and said, "Go see whose car that is out front."

My grandfather, who worked in a mill, cleaned downtown offices and drove a cab, all for his expanded family, was never one to be questioned, let alone disobeyed. So, I grabbed a robe and padded out to the curb. There sat a used 1974 Ford Maverick. It was clean as a whistle and totally empty, from the glove compartment to the trunk.

"There's nothing in it to let me know whose car this is," I said to him as he stood on the front porch near the front door.

"Now you can get to work," he said. And he turned and walked back into the house.

I stood in the street sobbing.

No, we were not a traditional family. But we were an intentional family. We were the family we needed, that I needed. We were not traditional. We were not a two-parent household with a mom and dad and sister and brother.

But that couple who raised their two daughters, then raised three of their grandchildren, was a power couple with stellar character, an out-of-this-world work ethic and humor when needed. They were loving, empowering and, more important than anything, they were there. And they were the best I could ever have had.

So dear hearts, do not let anyone define your family, whether you live with an auntie or your grandparents or with people who don't share your blood, but share your dreams.

Love the family you have and love yourself enough to make them proud.

All my best,

ROCHELLE

(Sister to hundreds of women who are not my sisters and "Mama Ro" to dozens of children who aren't my own)

....

DEAR LITTLE SIS,

Daughtering ain't easy. Can I say that?

We daughter. More than a relationship, it's a thing we do. We daughter.

We carry on our faces the reflection of our mothers. Her hopes. Her dreams. The parts of her she loves and fears the most. We daughter.

We bear the burden of her mistakes, her shames. We may even bear the marks of the pre-emptive beatings, meant to keep us from making mistakes we didn't even understand were possible. We daughter.

We see the world through our mothers' eyes. We hear life through our mothers' ears. We even hear our mothers' words echo from our own mouths. We daughter.

We carry our mothers: all of who they really were and were afraid of becoming, who they wanted to be and couldn't figure out how to be and who they couldn't figure out how to not be. Before we know who we are, our mothers become a template for our identity, our hopes, our futures. We daughter.

It takes a spiritual resilience to daughter. It takes intentionality of self-knowledge and radical love to daughter. To daughter, we must live: unraveling the giant myth of our mother that exists solely in our minds and finding beneath it who we really are.

Daughtering ain't easy.

I know my mommy loved me. Her momma loved her. And my mommy's grandmama loved my grandma.

I come from a line of women with strong, distinct personalities. Introvert. Extrovert. Tomboy. Girly girl. Science. Humanities. Nature-lover. Book lover. Artsy. Sporty. We are explicitly who we are. Our daughters are our opposites. My mommy is the outdoorsy, tomboy, science type. Her mother was a librarian whose mother was a farm-hand. My mommy had to stay inside, play the piano, sing, and read books. My mommy wanted to give me all the freedoms she didn't have and I love her for that. I played softball. Warming up before a game, the ball hit me in the face. My jaw was wired shut for 6 weeks. I tried to be a tomboy. I broke my wrist and all my toes. And I ripped up my favorite shirt: an ivory turtleneck with little purple hearts and lacy sleeves. I tried to garden. I freaked out when I got dirt on my hands. I ran inside when I saw a worm. My momma did put me in dresses. Blue dresses. And rubber-soled dress shoes so I could run. I don't run. She wanted me to be free. That wasn't freedom to me. Daughtering ain't easy.

I was 20 when I realized I could just be me. I fell in love with the philosophy my mom was forced to read. I built my own home library. I stopped trying to play sports. I was 30 when I realized I didn't have to walk in my mother's footsteps. I chose a life that makes sense to me. I refused to give up my dreams for the sake of stability.

I was 35 before I realized that I don't have to try to erase my mother's image from my skin—that seeing her in me doesn't erase me.

At 40, I still argue we look nothing alike. I wear pink and purple and ruffles and lace and play in makeup and have tattoos and I am decidedly myself. I still struggle to daughter. It ain't easy.

I hope you figure it out sooner, Little Sis. I hope you learn that your mother's choices in life were hers and not yours. I hope you learn how to emerge from your mother's image and reflection, and value your own. I hope you learn how to choose your own path, neither repeating nor running from your mother's past. I hope you learn how to value the differences between you and your mom. I hope you learn how to love your mom for who she is and how she loved you. I hope you learn how to hold loosely to her faith, her hopes, her dreams, her fears, choosing to keep what works best for you. I hope you grow into the woman you were meant to be—more than your mother's wildest dreams. I hope you learn how to live in your own skin, follow your own faith, carry your own hopes, chase your own dreams.

When you have a daughter, I hope you go easy on her and remember what it was like to daughter. Because we daughter and daughtering ain't easy.

BRANDEE

∙∙∙

DEAR LITTLE BLACK GIRLS I ONCE SAW IN A SOUTH DAKOTA WATER HOLE,

We were the only Black people at Evans Plunge Mineral Springs.

You were two pretty, dark-skinned girls splashing around the coldish water. You were tucked within a large white family and I was with my white boyfriend, driving cross-country between Portland and New York.

After an hour or so, our trio were the only ones standing within the echoing shower of the ladies' locker room. The droplets hit the ground like random applause, and you gazed at me with wide, cavernous eyes, neon bathing suits stark against the darkness of the room.

I smiled because I did not know what to say.

Almost eight years later and my mind still flutters towards you.

You are close to 12 now.

Dear Not-So-Little Black Girls I Once Saw in A South Dakota Watering Hole:

We are a different 12.

There are online forums for transracial adoptees. Four Black women were crowned the most beautiful in their universes just last year. There is a Black *Little Mermaid*. Maybe your parents learned to Bantu knot via a YouTube tutorial. Maybe they know colorblindness is not an attribute. Maybe they take focused care to gently lead you through this thing called life proud of being a Black girl.

We are the same 12.

A 12 teeming with questions unasked, because life is odd and dynamic. Like, why are white girls driven to make your life a passive-aggressive hell? Why were you given up anyways? Why do some

Black girls make fun of the way you talk? How can you be proud of yourself and admit that sometimes, everything is confusing?

I was once a Black girl fostered by white people. A young Black woman in schools that were mostly white. When I brought up instances of racism or sexism, I was told I was too sensitive, crazy, and/or my favorite: a class-A racist myself. Sometimes, the worst hurt was the ones I received from those who looked like me. I learned to bottle the storm, lock it in within my shoulders and stomach. Pretend.

Still.

I am here, loving this self. Liking her more days than not.

Dear now Not-So-Little Black Girls I Once Saw in A South Dakota Watering Hole:

There is a concept in yoga called *ahimsa*, which is a respect toward all living things and a practice of non-harm. Most people usually think of this topic as it relates to other human beings and animals, but when it comes to Black girls adopted or living in white places, the work of *ahimsa* is just as powerful when applied to the self.

We who too often learn to harm ourselves in ways the world will not recognize or care about. We who learn to suffer silently because there are bigger concerns.

I smiled at you that day, my mouth wordless. What I had wanted to say was:

Please do not hurt yourself.

Adore your skin, hair, your mouth, your heart and your mind. Never try controlling another human being. Accept the history of who you are and how you came to be. Practice love and respect.

The white girls who perform quiet meanness and the Black girls who tease you are dealing with a pain that is not yours to carry.

Do not try.

Dear Not-So-Little Black Girls I Once Saw in A South Dakota Watering Hole.

You will mess up.

I chose white dolls over Black ones, lived in an era where I thought white things were smarter, deeper, better. I quieted the essence of who I truly was around Black people, belittled my experience for the difference it held.

Ahimsa is a practice, a chain, a string of beads linking to infinity.

And life is life.

In that shower eight years ago, you stared like I was the first Black person you had witnessed in a long time. We regarded each other in the rush of water and steam, our flip flops squishing bubbles. If your eyes were silent X-rays, at the center of my chest would have been a prayer for you that had yet to be made into words.

Dear Not-So-Little Black Girls I Once Saw in A South Dakota Watering Hole.

May you love yourself exactly as you are.

And have the courage to always try.

Love,

HANNAH

Dear Beloved Black Girl,

As a kid growing up in the 1970s and 1980s, I watched a lot of TV. No, really, I mean, *a lot* of TV. We didn't call it binge-watching then, and for most of my childhood there were only three channels, with no shows on demand. But my friends and I still managed to watch hours of TV each day. Some of my favorite shows were ones about families with a mom and a dad. Not families like mine, with a mama and a grandma. My parents never married, and my father didn't live with me. I only saw him on occasion, and even then, most of the time he would pick me up and take me to his parents' house and leave me.

My favorite TV shows made me wish I had a normal family, with a normal dad. I wished my father lived with us. I wished he was around to give advice and go on vacations and keep his promises, the way a TV dad did. Or at least try to make it up to me when he broke his promises, the way a TV dad would. TV dads also didn't lie, drink too much, dodge child support, and live apart from all of their children.

I loved my father, but he made me feel ashamed. He was a deadbeat dad, a walking stereotype of the absentee Black father. If he was those things, I wondered as a kid, what did that make me?

I loved my father, but I was ashamed because he lied to a judge and said I wasn't his child, trying to avoid paying child support.

I was ashamed, even though I hadn't done anything wrong.

I felt lonely a lot as a child. My mama and grandma showered me with love and attention, but the hole in my heart was shaped like my father. I don't know what it's like to be a Daddy's Girl, or to have a father be proud of me and my accomplishments.

I loved my father, but I didn't start to have a relationship with him until the final months of his life. He died when he was 54 and I was 34.

I cherished those months, but I wish he would've been more present in my life when I was a child.

Maybe your dad lies too and doesn't keep his promises. Maybe he doesn't help take care of you. Maybe he isn't around to cheer you on at your games or make sure you've done your homework. Maybe you've lost count of the ways he's hurt you or let you down.

I've been there.

My mother pushed me to have a relationship with my father that he didn't want. She pushed me to respect him as a father, even though he did nothing to earn that respect.

I grew up in the church, and we were taught that the Bible says you must honor your father and mother. I wanted to be a good Christian, so I thought that meant I had to act like my father was a good dad, like a TV dad. I thought I had to keep forgiving him, even though he never asked for forgiveness or changed how he treated me.

As I got older, I found myself looking to boys to give me the love and attention I didn't get from my father. As an adult, I learned that this is common for girls like us, and it can lead to a lot of heartache and problems. If you're anything like me, you'll fall in love easily, equate sex with love (it's not the same thing!), choose boys who lie and are untrustworthy, and then be devastated when the relationships end. I know that trying to hold back the tsunami of teenage hormones and emotions is hard, especially when your dad hasn't been there for you, but I encourage you to take things slowly and choose wisely. Don't settle for someone just because you don't want to be alone. If you take one lesson away from this letter, let it be this: *It's better to be alone than to be with someone who doesn't treat you with kindness and respect, the way you deserve to be treated.*

And did I mention that sex and love are not the same thing? Okay, good.

Back to my father. As I got older, I was confused by his behavior. Why wouldn't he want to be there for me the way his father, my granddaddy, was there for him and his five siblings? My grandparents were married for more than 60 years. To my knowledge, my grandfather was always present. But now that I'm an adult, I understand that being there for your child means more than just physical presence. I don't know if my father experienced the kind of parenting that I needed from him as his child. I don't know if he knew how to be a good father.

Now that I'm almost 50, I can see my parents as not just my parents but as people. I can see them as people with their own trauma, fears, and grief, from when they were kids and as adults. I can see them as people who hurt and disappointed me, but who were also hurt and disappointed by others, including their parents. The fancy term for this is *generational trauma*. Unless we deal with it, we will pass down pain and bad choices from generation to generation. That's not to excuse my dad or your dad for the ways they failed to be the fathers we needed them to be. Generational trauma isn't an excuse, but it is an explanation that helps girls like us better understand the choices our parents made.

But understanding alone isn't healing. The kind of relationships we had (or didn't have) with our fathers impacts every aspect of our lives—how we see ourselves, how we see the world, who we share our lives with. So healing is important. I don't know the ways that your dad wasn't there for you. But I know that whatever happened, it wasn't your fault. And I know that your healing can begin there. Push past the shame. Tell someone you trust how you feel. Ask for help dealing with your feelings.

Therapy has helped me deal with my feelings about my father. Also, I've always loved to read, so I turn to books for healing as well. *The Fatherless Daughter Project* is a book that has helped heal my father-wounds. I didn't read it until a few years ago. I wish I had read it when I was your age.

Some people believe that forgiveness is required in order to heal. For them, that may be true. But I don't believe that's true for everyone.

Instead of being taught to honor and forgive a father who did not deserve it, I wish that as a child I had been taught to honor myself and my feelings. Forgiveness is complicated. We don't owe anyone forgiveness. We owe ourselves compassion and tenderness and time.

Don't let anyone pressure you to forgive your father. In fact, question everything, especially those things that require you to put other people's feelings and comfort before your own. Too often, people demand this of Black girls and women. They say we must be silent about our pain in order to "lift up" Black men, for the sake of the Black community. This is a lie, plain and simple. We must love ourselves first. Learning to love myself has helped me heal.

Today, I have two daughters, and they have a wonderful father. Thanks to him and other men I know, I've seen good Black fathers in action. I've seen the kind of love, care, and attention I deserved from my father—and that you deserve from yours. That absentee Black dad stereotype is just that—a stereotype. Research shows that Black fathers, married or not, are actually more active in their children's lives than other fathers.

Something else I've learned: There's no such thing as a "normal" family, and one family type isn't better than another. A family is defined by who is there for you, not who isn't there. The people who love and care for you, and who you can count on? That's your family.

And one final and very important thing I've learned: You aren't defined by how your father treated you. If he wasn't a good father, know that you deserved better. My hope for you is that you thrive in the world as someone who deserves love, respect, and honesty. Because you do.

Love,

DEESHA

··

Dear Powerful Black Girl,

Adoption. The word can be like a large, overstuffed suitcase with tons of compartments, filled with words like *negativity, abuse, uncertainty* and *confusion.* Regardless of what is in your suitcase as an adoptee, the depth and breadth of what's in it make the suitcase almost too heavy to move, let alone carry. And growing up I felt like I had these feelings of abandonment, lack of self esteem with no true place where I belonged and even the smallest slight or incident caused me to question my self worth.

Growing up a little Black girl rarely did I feel totally at peace. I had always known that I was a stranger in a strange land. The first time that I realized that I was "someone else's child," I was almost 5 years old. I remember clearly riding in the back of a car that someone I didn't really know was driving with my younger sister sitting beside me. I remember thinking that my life was changing in such a big way and that I was much too young to understand the fullness of it. I knew, even at that tender age, that all of this was without my permission. It was scary and I was powerless.

My sister and I were dropped off at the home of a single, middle-aged, Black woman in a notorious housing project in the south end of my city. I wouldn't know until much later how infamous my new "hood" was. From what I've been able to gather from court documents and piecing together stories from my biological family, things happened like this: When I was less than a year old, someone called the local children's services agency and reported that my siblings and I were being terribly neglected and abused. We were all severely underweight, and I had sores and hair loss due to lack of proper care for a skin rash I'd developed as a baby.

I compare my adoption story to Superman's. As a little baby named Kal-El, Superman's whole world literally blew up. Just moments before his home planet Krypton was destroyed, his parents put him in a small spaceship and sent him to Earth. He landed in Smallville, a stranger in a strange land. From a very early age, Superman knew he was different. He was stronger and ran faster than everyone else. He grew up to be the strongest, most powerful being on Earth! That's what I wanted to do also: Grow up strong so that I could carry around that suitcase of heavy feelings that had been dropped at my feet when I was placed in foster care.

And like Superman, questions about my origin story constantly swam around in my head and heart: Who am I? Where did I come from? To whom do I belong? What is my purpose? Do I even have a purpose? But unlike Kal-El, we Earthly adoptees are mere mortals who don't have a Fortress of Solitude to learn about ourselves. We are on our own.

Some adoption stories involve abuse: physical, psychological and emotional. But even when those markers aren't the reasons for the new life we adopted children find ourselves in, we still have to deal with people saying we should be grateful to have a family to help save us from our old lives and give us new lives. Just because family and youth services weren't involved in your foster/adoption story, it doesn't mean that you aren't affected. And it doesn't mean you don't feel loss or grief. Whatever your adoption story, you have a heavy suit-case to carry. Lay it down. Unpack it, and rid yourself of the pain and feelings of being unwanted. You too have a powerful story!

Joan, the woman who chose to foster, and later adopt, my sister and me never made me feel like I wasn't her biological child. It was other people's ignorance, intended and not, that continued to reinforce my sense of displacement. People would make offhanded comments about Joan's *adopted* girls.

Friends may ask if you feel lucky that a good woman or man or family took you in. The question I was asked most often was, "Do you

want to see your biological mother? Do you miss her?" My answers:
YES!! But also *HELL NO!!* and lots of responses in between. My
answers to that question were as complex as I am, and rarely did the
people asking these "innocent" questions understand their impact.

Now that I'm 43, here's what I've learned and here's what I want
you to know: YOU WILL BE ALRIGHT! As a matter of fact, you're
going to be more than alright. You're going to be great. Because you
will come to realize that there is more to your life than the decisions
your birth mother made to place you for adoption, if the decision was
even hers to make. And you are definitely NOT defined by rape, abuse,
neglect, bitterness, dysfunction, if any of these were factors in your
foster/adoption. You are also not defined by those who adopted you.
Those limiting beliefs are the things you remove from that suitcase.
What you keep in it is your parents' love for you! That may be hard to
see at first, but trust me it's there!

A part of you is the biological people who couldn't raise you; and
a part of you is the nurturing, support, compassion and dedication of
those who did raise you. I look just like my biological mother, and for
years, I struggled with that. But now I love my milk chocolate brown
skin, wide smile, small nose and high cheekbones. I found my love
of reading and my loyalty for those closest to me from Joan, who put
her all into raising me. There is the DNA that made me, and the envi-
ronment that shaped me. But I also have a destiny and purpose that is
wholly independent of both women.

As I sit and write this letter, there is sadness in my heart and tears
in my eyes, thinking about how some children have their origins in
this place of sadness. But I also feel excitement and joy because I know
that you don't have to remain in that place. And with tons of therapy,
self reflection, and God, I have learned to lay down my suitcase. Now
instead, I carry a more manageable (and fashionable) Burberry Hobo
bag. I sling it around my shoulders and pull from it confidence, pride,

compassion and love—all of the things that help me walk boldly in being MY BEST SELF!

Powerful Black girl, my wish for you is this: find your special bag. Maybe it's Burberry, or maybe it's one made for you by someone who loves you. Lay down your pain, bitterness, hurt and mistrust and start truly believing in your purpose and destiny. Ask your loved ones to help you.

You are here, in this time and in this place for a reason that is bigger than you may realize now! Like Superman you were meant to be strong, fast and powerful. Embrace it and fly!!

SHERRY

Dear Little Sister,

Relationships between a mother and daughter can be beautiful and challenging. For the past two years, my relationship with my mom has drastically changed. We went from talking almost daily and seeing each other often to sporadic text messages and face-to-face visits that mostly happen by chance. I used to feel like I was my mom's best friend, mother, therapist and more. There were times in recent years when I felt like we were barely acquaintances. This distance may have been the best thing to ever happen to us.

Two summers ago, I was confronted with two uncomfortable situations with my mother. One involving men and the other money.

One weekend I spent the night at my mother's house, and she had a male visitor stay the night. I am 30, but my mother's seemingly harmless act reminded me of when I was 10 years old and was awakened by the sound of her having sex. I cried. My mother came in my room, pulled my hair and told me to shut up. I never told her how much that hurt. But this night, as an adult, I spoke up. I told her that I was uncomfortable.

A few months later, my mother was in money trouble. I had asked her to sit down and make a plan to avoid expensive "emergencies" that forced me to come up with hundreds of dollars to rescue her from trouble. That was not a pretty conversation. I asked tough questions. And I will admit, my tone was not positive or comforting. My mother became emotional and I became detached. I was fed up with her tears and her messes and wanted to see her act like an adult and get her shit together. It hurt to walk away from her meltdown.

Having a strained relationship with my mother used to hurt so much. I had many sleepless nights and anxiety attacks. I felt like the worst fucking person on the planet. Why did I even say anything about her male friend staying the night? I had the money to fix her issue. Why didn't I just go to the ATM and make it okay? I shared with my therapist that I worried one of us might die without "fixing" things. But I love my mother and I wanted something different—a better, healthier relationship—for us. This period of separation was the key to my mother and I healing as women and as mother and daughter.

My mother had me when she was 17 years old. She told me many times that my arrival is what taught her about love. She grew up with an absent father, troubled mother and was shuffled between her older siblings' homes. She experienced different forms of abuse, including sexual and emotional. That lack of stability and nurturing my mother received as a Black girl affected our relationship. I believed it was my job as a daughter to make her happy and secure. I was extra careful not to displease her. I would not even wear an outfit or hairstyle that she didn't like. She made me feel like doing things my own way was a slight to her. I felt suffocated by the heaviness my mother carried around inside.

As I was growing up, my mom was super critical. She picked at herself and the world around her. I became very aware of the ways I was not perfect. What is a little Black girl supposed to think when she sees her mother [worry] over the smallest details—dust on the floor, food left on plates, every hair on her head—day in and day out? My mother always needed reassurance that she was good enough loved and capable. As an adult, I tried to give gifts, create experiences and do things to fix it. But nothing was ever good enough.

I could not make up for the ways that my mother was not mothered when she was a little girl. And the more I tried, the more I missed out on being mothered myself.

In the time my mother and I were distant, I opened myself to be mothered by the universe. I built loving relationships with friends who taught me to address conflict in a loving manner. I became closer to an aunt who would check on me every day and "kidnap" me for sleepovers full of good food and rum. I befriended a compassionate manager and "mothered" my beautiful cat Opal Marie. I began to see mothering and my mother in a new way. Like rapper André (3000) Benjamin once said, "I love who you are, love who you ain't."[1] My mother isn't perfect, and no mother is.

Two weeks ago, I got an unexpected job offer. The first thing that popped in my head was to text my mother. I told her that I needed her and wanted to hear her advice. Outside of being my mother, she is a woman with rich life experiences and wisdom to share. I was grateful to be able to talk with her, woman to woman, about what is going on in my life. Our relationship will never be the same. I don't want it to be.

I struggled for years to figure out who I was and how much of my mother I wanted to see when I looked in the mirror. As fate would have it, I see her more and more each day as my features morph into hers. At first it scared me. Now I see it as a blessing. Because my mother is, I am. I may not agree with her decisions and choices, but I can love her and be honest. I can love her and not carry the burden of making her feel loved. It is not my job to heal my mother. I have taken the scary steps to exorcise the trauma "demons" from my spirit, loosening the bind they've had on my family for generations. I allow my mother to do the same. By healing myself and learning to establish boundaries, I am actively loving my mother more than I ever have, without codependency and obligation.

Little sister, never forget to take care of you. It is the best thing you can do for those you love because it gives them permission to do the same.

Much Love,

BIG SIS E

—— *Know This* ——

ANCESTORS are the family who came before you—way back—like your great-granddaddy or great-great-great-grandmother.

BONUS MOM/DAD is a name for stepparents or other adults who play an "extra" parenting role in the life of a child. I am a proud bonus mom! I married a man with two great kids, and I was lucky to work alongside him and their mother to help them grow up.

FAMILY is traditionally defined as a group related by blood, ancestry, marriage, or adoption. But that definition can exclude people—for instance, queer girls who may have been rejected by their bio families, but still have people who love and care for them.

FAMILY OF CHOICE includes loved ones you select instead of just people you are related to closely by blood. For example, a family of choice can be a tight circle of friends or a bio family that embraces you as one of their own. Families of choice can offer all the love and unconditional support that a good bio family can.

GOTCHA DAY is the anniversary of a child's adoption and can be celebrated like a birthday or other special event. The day that a child joins a family through adoption is also sometimes called "Family Day" or "Homecoming Day."

PLAY COUSIN/AUNTIE/UNCLE is a common term in the Black community and refers to people who are not related by blood, marriage, or adoption, but are so close that they are given honorary family status.

Letter to My Black Girl Self

Who do you belong to? Who is guiding you? Whose rituals and customs will you carry on? Who holds you and holds you down? Who makes you feel safe? Who takes care of you? Who supports your dreams? Who do you laugh with? Who do you love? Who loves you? Who is your "tribe"? Write a letter about these people in your life—whether they are related by blood or love. This is your family.

CHAPTER 3

WHERE MY GIRLS AT?

Sisterhood

MY FRIENDS, REAL FRIENDS

Sometimes when I'm not sure how to talk about a Black girl thing, I consult the Book of Beyoncé, and sure enough, the Queen has said it for me in song. On the song "Friends" from the album *Everything Is Love* with hubby Jay-Z, Bey sings about her "friends, real friends,"

> They pray and pray for me, they pray and pray for me
> See better things for me
> Want better days for me unselfishly
> They pray and pray for me, they pray and pray for me
> Whenever I'm in need[1]

My girls ride for me like that. I ride for them, too.

When I was growing up, my girls played outside with me in the summertime until the streetlights came on. They passed notes to cute boys for me in high school. I studied with them all night in college. I listened to them cry over bad breakups and said, "He don't deserve you, girl." My girls rode cross-country with me, staying in cheap hotels, exploring towns off the highway, and laughing . . . always laughing. I cheer my girls on when they get new jobs and new babies, and when they do dope things. (And they always do dope things, because my friends are dope.) They stood up with me when I got married and turned up with me in a cabin in the woods when I turned 50. My girls helped edit this book. They told me when they thought I had captured Black girl stuff just right and when I had it wrong. Ain't no one on earth gonna love you like a Black girl. Periodt.

Black girl, the strength of your sister circle is a reflection of your love for yourself and other Black girls. Make sure you got some good Black girl love in your life. It will make your life richer and your journey much more fun. In the letters that follow, Black women will tell you how to find and keep great besties, ride or dies, and day-ones.

DEAR YOUNG SISTER,

Greetings! I hope this letter finds you well, safe, and full of joy. I have been pondering the importance of friendships in the lives of Black women lately and thought I would share my thoughts. Friendships with women have always been important to me because I am an only child. At some points in my childhood I longed for sisters and brothers, but mostly just sisters. I wanted someone to keep my secrets, play and trade clothes with, and love me unconditionally. I had a few cousins and church friends that I spent lots of time with. I not only loved these girls, I was LOYAL and would defend their honor by literally fighting for/with them if need be. I think there was a part of me that wanted them to see me as a "sister" more than a friend and I wanted to prove that I was worthy. As a teenager and young adult woman I realize now that many of the female friendships I cultivated were centered in my wanting to be liked, loved, and emotionally cared for; however in some of these "relationships" I was the only one doing those things. I made plenty of friends with women who did not have the capacity to love themselves appropriately and certainly could not be a great friend to me.

Over the last few years I have been challenged to think about female friendships and more specifically healthy female friendships. Healthy female friendships are only possible if both women are self-aware, emotionally/mentally stable, and committed to the relationship. These relationships have to be based on mutual respect, honesty, compassion, and desire to see the other person succeed. If you meet girls who talk about their other friends to you, trust me, they are doing the exact same thing about you. These are not the girlfriends you want or want to be. You want to be able to access all parts of your humanity in friendships with other girls, not being afraid that they will disparage your name to others. If you meet girls who loudly declare that they do not like girls and prefer friendships with boys, they have just told you all you need to know. Walk away. Those girls have usually been hurt by a friendship and have now internalized it as all girls are bad. Plus, if she doesn't like other girls that means she doesn't like herself much. You want to be in friendships with girls who genuinely love themselves and other girls.

A good friend is someone who shows up for you. She is going to call/text and check in regularly to make sure you are good. She is someone who has your back but can also tell you when you are strong and wrong. And when she challenges you it won't be in a nasty, hurtful way. You will leave the conversation with your dignity and feelings intact. She is going to applaud your successes and champion your causes as if they are her own. She is actively working to improve herself and encourages you to do the same. She has goals and dreams and works hard to achieve them. Both of you allow each other room to develop friendships with others recognizing that those relationships don't diminish your relationship. If you have an argument in a healthy friendship it doesn't get nasty and no one is bringing up personal information to hurt the other person. You both try to work it out and apologize if necessary to the other person. There is compassion, kindness, love, camaraderie, and fun in healthy female relationships. Each person should feel as though the other person genuinely appreciates all aspects of the other person.

I believe that racism and sexism have presented challenges in the formation of healthy friendships between Black women and girls. Racism has pitted Black women against each other via classism and colorism. Classism separates us based on how much money and education we have, the jobs we do, where we live and the culture we display. Some people aren't interested in being friends with others whose success in those areas doesn't mirror theirs. Feeling superior to girls who are different from you blocks opportunities for fruitful friend-ships. Colorism, a belief that light-skinned people are better and more attractive, has also complicated Black women's relationships. This construct was birthed out of slavery and the idea that lighter-skinned Black people were closer to being white and granted privileges that darker-skinned people were not. It has pitted us against our sisters and created deep long-lasting wounds.

Close friendships between Black girls and women are not only possible, they are needed. I cannot think of one situation, good or bad, that I haven't made it through without the love, support, compassion, laughter, kindness, and joy of my close Black "sisterfriends." We need each other to survive, literally. Be the friend you want because like attracts like.

Best~

LISA

....

My Dearest Young Sister,

I am deeply honored to have a few moments to spend with you during this stage of your life journey, as you make the transition from girlhood to womanhood. As you continue to evolve into the person that you want to be, there are going to be countless relationships that you will experience along the way and, in my opinion, some of the most significant relationships that you have will be with other Black women.

Despite what you may see on reality television or read on social media, Black women and girls are a lifeline for one another, more often than not. Here are a few examples from my own life:

When I was in elementary school, I was truly an awkward Black girl: I was taller than everyone (including the boys), I wore glasses, and I was much more bookish than athletic. With all of that going for me, I was teased. Daily.

All of that ended when I met PD. In today's world, she would probably be considered a bully, but for me, she was a protector. Whenever someone would start to pick on me, she would step in to defend me, with words or with actions. At a time when I lacked the confidence to speak up for myself, she became a powerful voice for me.

I grew out of my awkwardness (at least a little bit) and no longer needed a bodyguard, but I found a lifelong friend in PD, who will still go to bat for me if necessary.

In my 20s and 30s, most of my friendships developed out of shared experiences with other sisters: in college, at work, at church, in social groups, etc. Out of all the women that I called "friend" during those years, only a select few have managed to stand the test of time. The others were there for a season or a reason, yet I am still grateful for the part that each one of them played in my life.

In the last few years, most of my new friendships have resulted from meeting like-minded women in virtual settings or interest-based meetup groups. A couple of those new friends have collaborated with me for writing and speaking ventures. Another friend introduced me to an organization that has provided me with additional friendships, leadership opportunities, and lots of adventure. Yet another sister-friend has become both my sounding board and travel buddy. In all three cases, my associations with these women have expanded my horizons and enlarged my territory.

Now, I must admit that not every relationship that I have had with another Black woman has been positive: I have repeated things that I shouldn't have. I made promises that I couldn't keep. I have dated a friend's ex-boyfriend. I have ghosted people when things got rough instead of taking the time to have honest conversations. I have had the same things done to me.

I judged other women because of their looks. I have questioned another sister's intelligence or authority. I have expressed negativity about a woman's lifestyle choices. I have wondered, "Why her and not me?" I have also been on the receiving end of all of the above.

You will experience a lot of the same ups and downs in your own friendships, but I encourage you to hold space in your heart for healthy connections with other Black women. Even though we don't always get it right with one another, as the late poet Gwendolyn Brooks stated, "We are each other's harvest; we are each other's business; we are each other's magnitude and bond."

In other words, there will be times in your life when your tribe of sisterfriends will be the lifeline that sustains you when the rest of the world has gone crazy. Or the ones that rise with applause when you reach your goals. Or the folks who speak the truth in love when you need sound counsel. Or simply just the people that love you without conditions.

I can't tell you when or how you will find the women who will become a part of your tribe, but I can tell you this: In order to have the type of friends that you desire, you must be the type of friend that you desire—one who is loving, kind, honest, trustworthy, respectful, non-judgmental, supportive, fun-loving, and a good listener.

Here's to a life filled with sisterly love!

Your Big Sister,

MARCIE

....

DEAR BLACK GIRL,

There is a formula for true friendship:

True friends give. They don't always take.

True friends allow you to be your true self. They don't ask you to conform to who they are.

True friends celebrate your triumphs, not your defeats.

True friends are honest, but kind.

True friends give name to your pain. They don't call you names.

True friends save you from bad situations. They don't create bad situations.

True friends build you up. They don't tear you down.

True friends honor you as a person. And they make you feel honored to know them.

It is not asking too much to demand these things of your girlfriends.

You may be thinking, "I mean, yeah, sometimes my friends are messy. We fall out over dumb stuff. Sometimes they are jealous or I am jealous. Sometimes they talk about me behind my back. Oh, and yeah, I talk about them, too . . . a little . . . maybe a lot. Sometimes a couple of them act like they are better than me. But they're my *girls*! Forgive and forget, right?"

Black girl, what you will accept in relationships, including friendships, is often a reflection of how much you value yourself or how you behave as a friend. Inconsistent friends are often a sign that something needs to change. Sometimes people show up or show *out* based on the energy you put into the world.

You say, "I don't like people who gossip." But you are the gossiper. And you attract gossips.

You say, "People always take me for granted." But you constantly put yourself last and you teach others to put you last, too.

You say, "I want friends who celebrate me and give me grace." But you dwell on poor decisions and situations and ignore your wins.

Remember that building lasting and true friendships requires that you have integrity and that you be a true friend to yourself. You have to take responsibility for your happiness and know your worth.

And don't *ever* believe an inconsistent friend means that "females are too hard to get along with. They are jealous and bring nothing but drama." Sadly, I know you have heard this before. Anyone who tells you this has never experienced the value, sisterhood, respect and admiration of true friendship with other girls. The older us Black girls get, the more we realize there is nothing like the warm embrace of a true friend and no one will ever have your back like your "sistahs."

Black girl, learn to love, honor and value yourself and you will attract like-minded, true friends who will remind you that you are worthy of respect, worthy of honor and more than worthy to be loved.

With Love, Respect and in the Spirit of Sisterhood,

DEIDRE

∙∙∙

DEAR SISTA GIRL,

I don't know about you, but my girls are like my family. No. They ARE my family.

Being a Black girl in this society that we have—one that expects, assumes, begs, pleads, disregards, and admires so much of us—we have got to surround ourselves with people who will want the best for us and want us to grow with them (even if it's not the same journey). One of your jobs in a radical act of self-care is to decide who this crew around you is. This is going to be a thing you will get wrong some-times (be gentle with you when this happens but learn) but when you get it right, you will have people in your life forever.

I'll give you two instances where I went right and where I really went so very wrong. I'll start with the wrong because I like to end with a good story. It starts with a boy. I know. But it did start with a boy that I thought I loved tremendously. At the time I thought he was wiser than me, he was intoxicating, he was mysterious and smart. When he looked at me, the sun just shifted right in my direction. And when he didn't pay attention, I was putting myself in a dungeon. So you understand this is not love. This is infatuation mixed with a little (or a lot) of self-esteem deprivation. But this isn't about him entirely. It's really about me being friends with one of his family members—this girl became like my sister because I liked her and, well, because I felt like if I didn't, I was done being in this boy's orbit. She made it easy. She was funny, generous, seemingly loyal, adventurous, and available. Our friendship began with our love of sarcasm and joy. We could hang out without saying a word sometimes and I was told that a quality like that was valuable. This went on for many years. But then cracks came. She began to emulate the hot and cold behavior of that boy I thought I loved. I would hear small things she said about me from others but

I wrote it off. She repeated criticisms that the boy would give me as though they were her own. She would tell me things about the boy that I really didn't want to know since he wasn't my man. I just loved him, I thought. But she introduced information about other girls as though I knew I was one of many, of things he did with other girls, and other things that she knew would hurt me. I didn't have the language to articulate what was happening or why. I mean we were friends and friends don't do that. Do what? What specifically could I beef about? It took years of journaling and conversations with myself to learn that manipulation comes in all kinds of bodies. People do things because they can. People hurt you because they are hurt. She snuck past what I thought were my obvious barriers against what I thought was so right and wrong.

What broke us was a fight while I was in London on vacation. I don't know what started it but I realized at some point when we were escalating towards her hurling insults at me along with super painful accusations (any time somebody comes at you in an argument with, "That's why you . . ." just walk away—nothing good comes after that), that she was not my homegirl. We were fighting via email during a time she knew was important to me and she didn't care. She spewed her venom and I stood my ground. Weeks later she apologized but the damage was done. She had shown me herself, even if it took a few years for her to do it. Nothing felt better than me telling her, "Look, my self-care prevents me from being around you. It's too much. Best of luck." I risked alienation and awkward mutual friend gatherings but honestly, it was all worth it. And the boy? Well, they were related in mannerisms and he got cut off too. I don't even care it took forever.

Now for the good story. The one where I was smart enough to collect a homegirl who would be like family. I was nearly 20 in my first waitressing job in New York. It was a popular restaurant that was on its way down. I was the youngest on staff but I had to work to put myself through school and this was just one way to do that. Marcella, the hostess, was about 10 years older than me and was a single mom to a five-year-old girl. At some point during the end of the shifts, a few of us would go to a diner. And since I lived far, she'd either let me sleep at her house or make me call her when I got home. First, we started with our love of music that wasn't typically Black like Sting or Hotel Costes. Then we talked about books. And then we talked relationships. She had really been through it. She shared with me some tough times but I was so young that some of it was lost on me. But she talked to me like I would know which parts of the story were important.

I want to break here and tell you that most meaningful relationships are a courtship even if they aren't always romantic. You are feeling each other out. You are sharing. You are discovering interests that bond you. Fully embrace that.

Marcella took an active interest in me as I was basically raising myself in my adulthood. I had outgrown my own mom in some areas. She couldn't help me with the new things I was experiencing living on my own in a new city. Marcella taught me how to have a household budget (a spreadsheet I STILL have today), how to consider how I feel in situations rather than allowing them to happen to me, how to stand up for myself, how to embrace creativity exploration (it's not just enough to have talent   you should put it out there to see where it goes), and how to guard my privacy (she is so private, she might as well be a secret agent to some). But the big thing that turned into many big things? One day she suggested we go to Italy. My first international trip ever. BLACK GIRLS IN ITALY! It was so on. She had been before but she told me it was time for me to see the world. That one gesture—a trip together—opened up a door of myself that I have yet to close. I saved up, got my first passport, and we went—discovering that we could be travel homegirls too! We learned we could give each other space, be excited about some of the same things, explore places we hadn't considered, and have a blast doing it all.

You see, Marcella helped me by exposing her own growth and allowing me to see that as a way of exploring my own. She did that on purpose. That is a gift. We have been sharing journeys ever since. It has been nearly 20 years. She has been at EVERY important moment in my life. She even officiated my wedding in Paris—a pop up in an opera house with a total of five people—including me and my husband.

The lesson is that a homegirl is going to give to you and let you give to her. You will not need to talk every day though sometimes you might. You may not even see each other regularly but you will feel like you do. Radical self-care is making sure that you have a homegirl in your life that you know can step in and take care of what needs to be done when you cannot and someone for whom you would do the same. This is not unlike your partner in life—whoever that may be. You are a person who gives so much to others even if you don't realize when you are. This means you have so many parts of you that deserve attention and respect as well.

Collect your people wisely.

TARA

——*Know This*——

BULLYING is unwanted, aggressive behavior directed toward someone with less power (size, physical strength, popularity, etc.). Sometimes intraracial bullying can happen between Black girls because of colorism, differences in class, or expressions of Blackness. For instance, a girl may get bullied because of the darkness of her skin, access to expensive things, or a way of speaking that is perceived as different from those around her.

DAY-ONE FRIENDS are friends that have been with you since your early days.

RIDE OR DIE in hip hop originally referred to a woman willing to do anything for her man—even things that are dangerous or illegal. She will ride with him and die for him—no questions asked. This is not—I should point out—healthy. The term "ride or die" has expanded, though, to refer to anyone who is willing to stand beside you through tough times. Your closest, most trusted girlfriends can be called your "ride or dies."

SISTERHOOD is a special positive bond formed between women and/or girls based on our shared identity and experiences.

Letter to My Black Girl Self

Black girl, the strength of your sister circle reflects your love for yourself and other Black girls. Write *two* letters. In one, write about how you can prepare yourself to be a good friend to other Black girls. In the second, write about how you would like to be treated (and not treated) as a friend. You attract the best friends by being a good friend. But friendship is a two-way street and you must understand your boundaries and be clear about the treatment you expect and deserve.

CHAPTER 4

WORK, WORK, WORK

Career and Other Passions

DO WHAT YOU LOVE

What do you want to be when you grow up? Many times, when people ask a girl that question, they mean, "How will you make money?" "What will your job be?" My dear Black girls, I hope you can think more deeply than that. What interests you? What gives you boundless joy when you do it? Do you love little kids? Do you like solving complex problems? Do you enjoy helping people? Do you like to travel?

According to Gettysburg College, adults spend one-third of their whole lives working—that is ninety thousand hours![1]

That time goes by much more quickly if you choose a career that incorporates some of the things you love. But you know what, Black girl, being able to do that is a privilege. Some Black women have to work at jobs they don't care for, simply to keep the lights on and their families fed. There is no shame in that. But know that the more you plan and the more you learn, the better your chances of having what you do when you grow up be a thing you really love and that suits you.

Also know that "what you want to be" is not simply about your 9-to-5 or 11-to-7. Your life is bigger than your career or job. For instance, "what you want to be" refers to your passions and your hobbies, too. I am an executive at a not-for-profit organization. I am also a writer. I was writing long before anyone ever paid me to do it or allowed me to write books. I wrote because I love playing with words. I wrote "books" even when I was a little Black girl. If you are lucky, your career and your passions will align, but the job that pays the bills may not be able to contain all the things you love. Make time for them, anyway, if you are privileged enough to be able to do so. For instance, my mother is a teacher, but she is also an excellent cook who frequently takes classes—even in other countries—and tries new recipes. She says indulging these interests makes her life richer.

In the letters that follow, Black women share how to set your goals for "when you grow up" and how to turn your passion into your livelihood.

....

DEAR LITTLE SIS,

Wait, I realize you don't know me, so maybe I am being a little too forward by calling you "sis." You see, I am the oldest of three kids and the only girl. I always dreamed of writing to you. I have waited decades to drop you some gems about life, the future of work, and what that means for people who look like us. I have been waiting for just the right opportunity to tell you all the things I wish someone had told me. Often, I wonder if I had received a letter like the one you're reading, maybe I would have been more prepared for the "real world." Maybe I would have known and believed that brown-skinned girls really do have skin like pearls like Beyoncé said. Let this letter always be a reminder on the days when you start to question your worth, that you are the prize in every room you walk into. They notice you! Matter of fact—YOU ARE THE ROOM!

When I was your age, I didn't realize how much power I possessed. I used to think I needed to shrink walking into boardrooms where I found myself as the "only" one—the only Black woman and sometimes the only Black person, full stop. And along the way, I picked up the bad habit of modifying and erasing my authentic self, in order to mirror what I thought the majority wanted from me. Like changing my name to something "easier" or more "palatable." Or wearing my hair in a certain style that didn't reflect the real me. Today, I finally get the chance to tell you that your work, career, hobbies, and love—all of it matters. There is a unique slice of brilliance that only you bring to every project and workplace. May you find power in the words that roll off your tongue when you advocate for yourself. May you find strength in the moments when you ask for more! And when you're feeling like running towards your fears, lean into your courage; because you will always be your best advocate.

Oh, and never be afraid to say no, to the people, places, and things that no longer serve you, so that you can make room for all of the times you want to say "Yes!" Life is so much sweeter when you say yes to the people, places, and things that bring you joy. You have the power to choose the authentic version of you, be it she, they, or them. This letter is for you, the little sister that I always wanted. As your big sis, I am here to let you know there are tables with a seat waiting for you with your name on it. Or you might decide to create your own table so that you can add seats for women like us. The sooner you learn that you will always need a squad of others, the better off you will be—because success is not a solo sport.

As you embark on the next journey of your life, there might be people who don't "see" you, but you must never forget that you have royalty inside your DNA. And as you secure your seat at the table, remember to breathe, keep your head high, and remember what our ancestor Audre Lorde said, "beware of feeling like you're not good enough to deserve it." And, when you get to be my age, I hope you will consider writing a similar letter to our little sisters that are coming behind you—let's make the workplaces and spaces better than we found them. I am rooting for you!

With love,

MINDA

DEAR BLACK GIRL!

Have you hidden a part of you from the world? Refused to speak your dreams out loud for fear that others will laugh at or discourage you? If so, I've been there too and can tell you it will be alright. You don't have to be the best when you start this journey. And there is no age limit to start. There is no correct way of following your dreams. You simply must make the choice and then start down that path.

I am an accidental artist. I didn't grow up making art. I didn't live in a community that said the arts were important. Living primarily in a rural area for many years, I can't even tell you when I picked up an art book or went to an art museum. For me, the world of art was connected to a PBS show called "The Joy of Painting with Bob Ross" and the handicrafts made by my great-grandmother—quilts, crochet, ceramic figures of angels and garden gnomes. That pretty much summed up my exposure to the arts.

Fast forward and years after becoming a full-fledged adult, I found myself friendless in a new city after moving across the country with $700 in my pocket to start "a new life." I took a painting class at the local art school at night to meet folks and scratch an intellectual itch. It was a figure painting class. This was completely backwards from the traditional way many artists are taught—first drawing objects, then drawing people, then painting objects, then painting people (the figure). So not only did I have zip skills in painting, I was starting this art journey completely backwards.

That first painting was a complete horror show. I didn't care. After the first class, I was completely and utterly hooked. I had found the "thing" that had been missing from my life.

For years I went to that art class after work until one day, my instructor told me that I needed more than she could offer. She sent me to a new teacher at the local college. "You have potential," he said. And for the next four years I worked all day and went to art school at night four days a week. In time, he too said it was time to move on. I then took the leap of faith and applied for graduate school.

Many said I wasn't ready—I wasn't good enough—in their own sly ways. It would sound like this, "Well, if you think *that* type of work will get you into graduate school." "Hmmm . . . *you're* applying for grad school? *That* grad school?" All of that is code for "not you." Others helped me figure out the process and present my work in the best way possible. I got in and never regretted that decision. Yes, looking back I can see where I needed to learn a little bit more in certain areas. But life is a process, a journey. Not an absolute. Skills can be learned over time. Opportunities must be taken when they present themselves. When I set out on this journey of graduate school, I wanted to see what it meant to be an artist. Where would this path take me? I knew I only had this one shot in life to give it a try and I took it.

So, what is the moral of the story? This is not one of those "pull yourself up by the bootstrap" stories. Those stories are full of it. This is not one of those, "If you try, it will all work out" stories either. Those are full of it, too. This is a story about taking a leap of faith and giving yourself a shot at whatever you are passionate about. I won't tell you that it will always work out. Or, that it will work out the way you think. But it does mean that you will not spend your life regretting your shoulda, coulda, wouldas.

I've never said my path has been easy or that there have never been times when I have questioned the choice. I am human after all and questioning is a part of the human journey. But the one thing I have never regretted is giving myself a chance to build a future I could believe in. So, seize the day and take a chance on you.

Good luck beautiful Black girl!

LaShawnda

DEAR BLACK PRINCESS,

You've been on my mind recently, and I wanted to take a few minutes to share some things that I have been thinking about. Some things that I wish had been shared with me when I was your age. So, I invite you, Black Princess, to grab your favorite coffee or tea, soda or water and spend a few minutes with me.

First, I want to tell you that I see you. That I appreciate you. That I love you and honor you. And that God loves you, too. I know that sometimes it feels as though you don't hear that enough. It feels sometimes as though society is telling your white sisters how amazing they are and forgets to tell you the same. Or how sometimes it feels like pulling teeth for someone to recognize your beauty and grace, your kindness and humor, your eyes . . . or the way you just *sway to the beat of your favorite song* the way that only you can. The way you're good at math and science (or not), the way you can sing, dance and act (or not), or the way you're really creative and good with your hands (or not). You see, it all matters.

Society may be telling your white sisters that they can be anything they want to be in this life, but sometimes it forgets to tell you that. No matter how much money or education you have, or how well-spoken or talented you are, your road will always be more difficult. The beauty is that these challenges will make you stronger. More resilient. And more empathetic than some of your white sisters. And for that, be grateful.

Sometimes, you just want it to be easy. You don't always want to learn the hard way. You just want things to come to you without resistance . . . and that is natural. But where there is ease, there are no lessons. Where there is no resistance, there is no growth.

I wrote a book for women called *Flourish: Have It All Without Losing Yourself,* and I shared several lessons that you, Black Princess, can use as well. First, the definition of flourish is to "grow luxuriantly." How cool is that, right? And there are six dimensions to flourishing:

Success. This is your work and your wealth. I will repeat what you've been told before—work hard, work smart, and work consistently. But you may not have been told to find a mentor, sponsor and champion to help you along the way. They will give you tools you can use, keep you on the right track, speak for you when you're not in the room, and provide another set of eyes to make your projects improve. They provide a challenge—now do you see why that is a good thing, as long as they do it from a place of love?

Self-Care. This is how you take care of yourself, but it is not just about eating your broccoli and doing your yoga—at least not just that. It's about how you manage stress and how much sleep you get. It's about *really* taking care of yourself. And in order to take care of yourself, you have to know yourself.

Spirit. This is an area that is near and dear to my heart. This is not a religious distinction, it's just about making sure that your spirit of gratitude and mindfulness becomes part of your daily routine. Make sure you find something larger than yourself (for me, that is God) to find peace and love and fellowship. And that you build a relationship with your God and yourself that is spiritual and based in love.

Synergy. This is about your relationships. Starting from those closest to you, to your classmates, work colleagues, and all the way out to the community and/or the world. Each person is valuable, so those whom you love, make sure you invest the time and energy to communicate with them, to earn their trust, and to be emotionally responsible for yourself. Emotional responsibility is owning your emotions and identifying that they are in fact yours. *You own your emotions.* All of them.

Service. Becoming a servant leader is a great way to flourish at any age. The 10 principles of servant leadership are a) Listening; b) Empathy; c) Healing; d) Self-awareness; e) Persuasion; f) Conceptualization; g) Foresight; h) Stewardship; i) Commitment to the Growth of People; and j) Building Community.

Legacy. What will you be remembered for 25 years after you leave this earth? That is what your legacy will be. Make sure it reflects your values, what you believe is important and the contribution you want to leave for generations to come.

I hope you'll take these lessons with you as you move forward in life. It doesn't matter what mistakes you've made in the past. What matters most is how you take the lessons from the past and use them to make the world around you a better place because you were here. You can do this and so much more. Keep flourishing!

I love you, Black Princess. Always.

RACHEL

——*Know This*——

BLACK NAME BIAS has been confirmed by research showing that job candidates with Black or "ethnic" sounding names (think Lakisha versus Madison) are less likely to be called for interviews.

GLASS CEILING is the invisible barrier created by racism, sexism, and other biases that can keep women and people of color overall from being promoted to positions of power in the workplace.

NATURAL HAIR BIAS is the negative perception against nappy, kinky, highly textured hair. Many people believe that hair commonly associated with white women—straight, fine, and silky—is more acceptable than hair and styles associated with Black women. Some employers require that Black women change their natural hair—cut locs, straighten Afros, and remove braids—to appear more professional.

WAGE GAP refers to the fact that women overall earn less than men for doing similar work. The wage gap is impacted by race, too. Black women make sixty-two cents for every one dollar earned by white men.

LETTER TO MY BLACK GIRL SELF

What is your passion? To organize? Teach? Solve problems? Find your passion and develop it, and your life will be richer. Your path will be clearer. Write a letter about your passion and how you can develop it as you grow. Include a list of women who do the thing that you hope to do and how you might learn from them.

CHAPTER 5

I DIDN'T ASK FOR THIS

Tough Stuff

THEY ARE WRONG ABOUT YOU

Even if you have a family that actively loves and affirms you, Black girl, outside you get bombarded with negative messages. You're going along, minding your business, feeling cute and smart, and—bam!—some one-hit rapper or baller says something grimy about Black girls. (I'm looking at you, Kodak Black.) Or you watch a friend get in trouble at school for wearing "too short" shorts when all the white girls around her have on the same thing. Or maybe you make a bad decision—you talk back to your dad or have sex too soon or get into a fight. Maybe something bad happens *to* you—you are a victim of assault or other violence. Maybe you begin to worry that "they" are right about Black girls, with all their negative, fixed ideas. Maybe they are right about *you*.

No! They are wrong. They are wrong. They are *wrong*.

But there is something about the wrongness society assigns to Black girls that can leave you feeling bad and guilty about common mistakes and things that aren't your fault or that are okay for other people who aren't Black and girls. And, in our guilt, we isolate ourselves. We hide our scars and traumas from view. We hide what we think is "wrongness." We feel alone.

You are not alone.

In the letters that follow, Black women share how they have navigated tough stuff like poverty, teen pregnancy, incarceration, and assault. You will learn that your sisters have faced your obstacles before and survived. You will learn, in the words of attorney and criminal justice reform advocate Bryan Stevenson, "You are more than the worst thing you have ever done."[1] You are more than the worst thing that has ever been done to you. You are more than your present circumstance.

You are not wrong. You are hope and promise for tomorrow in Black girl skin.

GOOD EVENING DARLING,

I write this letter from a hotel room in Houston, Texas, a long way away from my small apartment on Halsted Street in East Orange, New Jersey. I don't think, even as a child, I imagined a world bigger than that town full of hopeful hopelessness. I couldn't see past the concrete or crack needles that lined the path to where I now find myself today.

But here I am, writing to you my darling. I am writing you, wishing you well in a time that may seem to be anything other to little girls that look like you—that look like us.

I write you without knowing your story or your path, so perhaps I should share my own? I was the young flower that bloomed from the broken glass and concrete of the hood.

The daughter of the genius welder and engineer turned crack addict. He died before I could appreciate his brilliance. I am the child of two parents infected with HIV before there were medications to treat it. One died, the other is still here although forever changed.

The daughter of a valedictorian and woman in STEM who was accepted into every Ivy League she applied to, however, the isolation of being educated in a predominantly white school took its toll and she left too soon.

My mother studied biomedical engineering. I am now the Vice President of Strategy leading engineers in healthcare technology and I am owning my space to ensure your experiences won't be the same.

Life is complicated and nonlinear, learn that now. There are many paths to the same destination so if you should find that "Plan A" fails, remember to fall back on the rest of your alphabet.

I was a high school dropout but plan to soon begin my doctorate in Learning Technologies. Sometimes it's hard to catch my breath and take this journey in because there was a time when I thought that only people who held "Dr." as a title were physicians, but in a few years, I'll be one.

I am now one of 125 women chosen by the largest scientific organization in the United States (AAAS) to nationally represent women in science, technology, engineering and mathematics as an IF/THEN Ambassador, and in a few short months a life-sized statue of myself and 119 other incredible women will be on display and I will be thinking of you during its unveiling.

When you are low and feeling down and your body and energy are weary, remember these words. Pull from me all the positive energy I hold for you here in my heart as I type these words. Remember that within those veins, you carry the legacy of a dozen generations waiting for you to arrive to your own occasion.

Do not fear your own brilliance and beauty. Do not hide it or dim your light because others complain of the glare. If you feel like you are bigger than something, that's because you are.

I wish I would have written you from the beaches of St. Lucia or from the waters of Loch Ness in Scotland. I wish I could've taken notes during my commute to work in Silicon Valley or during lunch breaks while looking out on the bay in San Francisco. I wish you could walk with me through the buildings of Houston Community College as I work with the brilliant minds of the most diverse city in the nation to tackle the issue of flooding and climate change with technology. We should've been pen pals a long time ago, I'm sure there would've been much to discuss.

But know you were **there** with me.

Know you are **here** with me.

Know that you will be there for every keynote address at any given tech conference. You will be there for every new concept or application I create. For every new breakthrough, every algorithm, every data model created. You will be on my mind as I research while pursuing my doctorate to understand how you think and learn so someday someone can teach your children better than others have taught you.

Know that you are not alone.

You are not invisible, I see you.

You are capable.

You are powerful.

You are worthy.

You are a part of a larger community and with us, you are home.

As black women, we are not the exception—we are the norm.

And I will wait for you . . .

We will wait for you.

I will build an infrastructure for you and keep the path lit on your journey, so you'll never have to worry about finding your way again.

In moments when life seems most uncertain and you are most afraid of your future, think of the caterpillar who did not know that when it saw a butterfly flying above, it too would soon become one.

You are a part of something bigger, so accept the uneasiness in your gut when you desire more and trust it and then rise to your own occasion and you will be met with equal company.

NICOLE

DEAR BLACK GIRL,

I am writing this letter to help you not just survive but thrive. I hope that you will not be one of the Black girls who is disproportionately affected by sexual assault or violence, but the probability is that you, or someone you know or care about, will be subjected to one of these crimes. As a young woman, I was assaulted, and while I have been able to build a life for myself, it has not been easy.

First, it is not your fault. Do not let anyone convince you otherwise. It doesn't matter what you wore or didn't. It doesn't matter if you were intoxicated or sober. It doesn't matter if it was daylight or late in the evening. You, sweetheart, are not to blame. You were victimized by someone who sought to assert their power over you and dominate you in the way that may affect you physically, psychologically, and emotionally.

I am not going to talk to you about pressing charges, or how to engage the criminal justice system. While that can be part of your healing, it is an individual choice that only you can make. What I am going to tell you is that you can return to wholeness—in body, mind, and spirit—but that it will take time.

It wasn't easy for me. I blamed myself for trying to be grown. I blamed myself for going to a college party and separating from my friends—though it was only to use the restroom. I blamed myself for consuming alcohol at 17 although I was a college student and was just doing the same things that everyone else was. I will not share with you the details—the ones that I remember—but I will tell you that I woke up in my dorm room feeling horrible from head to toe. I didn't know how I had gotten back there, but I was grateful to be there.

Unlike now, where sexual assault is discussed more openly, I didn't have the resources available to me that are common now. While the campus health center talked about safe sex freely, they were really just beginning to talk about assault in that way. Who was I going to go to especially since I blamed myself? So, I kept it in. I kept it in and I spiraled out of control. Once a promising student, my grades plummeted. I'd stopped going to class and said "everything is fine." None of my friends knew and I wasn't going to tell them. I was succumbing to depression, something else that our communities didn't talk about. By the time the semester was over, I was on academic probation, and rather than tell the truth about why, I told everyone that I needed a break.

The week before I left campus, I finally visited the crisis center and told my story. Something made me want to have this on record. The counselor was fully understanding and since I was still a minor, asked if she could speak to my mother. I gave her permission. This way I didn't have to do it. When I returned home, my mother was in disbelief. Then, I thought that she thought I was lying to make up for my academic failures, but I know now that she felt guilt and shame for not being able to protect me. Her way of helping included getting me into group therapy as soon as possible, which helped at first.

Like many other survivors, I didn't want to really deal with the ramifications of my assault. There was still something telling me it was my fault. I went to therapy, smiled, and pretended that everything was ok, but it wasn't. It was eating me inside. Like the lyrics to Solange's song, Cranes in the Sky, "I tried to drink it away . . . dance it away . . . [I] sexed it away . . . read it away . . ."[2] There was the public me that was affable, funny, a great conversationalist, and the private me who wrestled with what had been done to me.

I couldn't keep up this duality much longer and at my core, deep in my spirit, I knew that I was worth something. I was valuable, regardless of what happened to me. I deserved to be free. It took me moving away from home, dropping out of another college, and really being with myself to get me headed in the right direction. Let me be clear, healing is not linear. There is no straight line from pain and damage to complete health. There would be weeks and months where I would be fine and on track, then something—a relationship, a song, thinking I saw one of the people who assaulted me—would trigger me and I would fall back into unhealthy patterns and coping mechanisms. That's ok. We are human and to be human is to be imperfect.

Through therapy, reading, and living my life as authentically as I could, I came to really understand that my attack had nothing to do with me. Sexual assault is never about the person victimized. Never. However, we make it about us because society/culture thrives on victim blaming. It allows people to never really be self-reflective and explore the ways that they cause harm. Hopefully, this is changing. Hopefully, the rates of sexual assault will decrease.

Being assaulted is not who I am. It is part of my life experience. Because I wanted to heal, I had to lean on some things I knew and learn some things I didn't. I had to re-learn that I am a human that is worth care and has value regardless of anyone else's ideas of me. I had to recognize that there is a higher power—call it whatever you want—but there is a force greater than me that wants me to be happy, healthy, and whole. I had to find the tools and resources that worked for me, which included group and individual therapy, and I had to take it one day at a time.

Am I still triggered? Yes, but not deeply. I don't watch or listen to anything that props up sexual violence. I've had to create those boundaries for myself and you will have to create whatever boundaries you need. Some will paint you as a bad guy for establishing your space, but in the end, it really is all about you and nourishing yourself back to health. As I grew to recognize that I am worthy, the shame and guilt around the assault began to disappear. Again, it doesn't happen overnight, but it can and does happen.

I want to leave you with this: you have the power to re-take control of your life after sexual assault or violence. You are not a victim; you have been victimized. Do not hold it in and pretend that everything is alright, because it isn't. Contact a treasured friend or family member. Use one of the many hotlines, such as the National Sexual Assault Hotline at (800)-656-4673. Get the help you need and begin the work that you need to heal.

As for me, I finally returned to college, got a BA, MA, and then a PhD. I married, had a wonderful daughter, and do work with young women and girls. Is my life perfect? Not in the least, but it's good and I love it because I have done (and continue to do) the sometimes hard, dirty work of loving and centering myself in a world that would rather not see me thrive, and you can too. I love you.

AIESHA

....

Dear Bad Ass Mama!

Twenty-two years ago, I walked across the stage and received a college degree in journalism with my mom and dad cheering me on. I walked off that stage and right into a job, working as a researcher for *The Oprah Winfrey Show*. (I know, right? I even got to be Oprah's hand model!) I left there and went on to graduate school. I finished in 18 months and packed my bags for Phoenix, Arizona, where I worked for a TV station, the local newspaper and a community college. Since then, my career has taken me across the country and around the world. I met President Barack Obama's grandmother, Mama Sarah, in Kenya. I've won three Emmy Awards for my skills as a TV news producer. I've worked for one of the world's largest pharmaceutical companies as a global public relations leader. I've been a college professor. And I co-founded an organization that teaches girls like you to be entrepreneurs.

Sounds cool, right?

I need you to know that when I was 16, most people doubted I would do any of this. In fact, they didn't believe I would even finish high school.

You see, when I was 16, I was curious about what sex felt like. So I tried it with a boy I thought I loved. I ended up pregnant. (And, later, he would end up going to prison for 13 years after committing a crime.) I was so ashamed and scared that I hid it from my parents until I was six months along—a terrible decision that was dangerous for me and my baby girl.

When they found out, my parents were disappointed, but they embraced us, protected us and loved both me and their first grand baby unconditionally. Not everyone else did, though. One thing that happened back then I will never forget. I was invited to be on a talk radio show for a segment about teen pregnancy. I sat there and listened while people called in and berated me and the other girls. We were called failures, welfare cases, hoes . . . every awful name you can think of. They pretty much said that we were the reason for every problem in the Black community. Another time, a friend of my family gave my parents a book for me about being a Black, poor, single mother. He said it would help me to better understand my future.

Too often Black girls like us are led to think we are less than— especially when we make big mistakes. Don't you ever, ever believe that. Your mistakes don't define you and they don't have to end you. When I would cry to my mother about how people treated me as a teen mom, she told me something I will tell you. She said, "Listen to what they're saying, but do not take their words to heart. Make liars out of them."

That's what I did. You can do it, too.

Being a young, single mom is hard. There were times when I couldn't pay my light bill. And when the lights went out, I'd used flashlights to give me the light I needed to finish my papers in graduate school. And I'd tell my daughter we were having a slumber party. She loved it! There were times when I had no car, so in order to get my daughter to school, I rode her on the back of my bike. There were times, when I was working the overnight shift in Phoenix, that my daughter would sleep beneath my desk, because I had no other place for her to go. There were many times, when I had to rely on the kindness of strangers to help, and I would pray those strangers wouldn't wrong us. I learned that it was always okay to ask for help.

This all seems like a long time ago now.

My little girl—the daughter of a teen mom—is all grown up and a mom herself. She is thriving as a fashion designer, making women feel beautiful in vibrant custom-made dresses and skirts. I am proud of her and proud of me.

The work. The tough road. The hardships paid off. My baby girl turned out okay. And the triumphs, the laughs we shared, the lessons we learned while we were growing up together brought us so close that we are inseparable now.

No. It will not be easy. But you deserve good things. Your baby deserves good things. You both deserve love. You can still achieve the goals you set for yourself and your family. Work hard. Ignore the haters. Other people's limited vision for you does not have to be your vision.

Go out and be great, mama!

With love, power and prayer,

DeShong
(Fellow Bad Ass Mama)

Dear Black Girl,

I hope this letter finds you well. I'd be lying if I said I haven't been struggling with writing it for the last several days. Even now, as a Gen Xer in her early 40s with a husband and a child and a life of her own, the ghosts of assaults past stay with me.

Two years ago this month, I was sexually assaulted by an acquaintance who offered me a ride home. My ex-boyfriend's cousin. Even at my big age, I pointed the finger at myself for not knowing better. Despite all evidence, despite knowing that the only way to prevent a rape is by not being a rapist, I still chastised myself for not doing enough to protect myself.

If you're of a certain age, chances are you've already experienced someone taking liberties with your body without consent. It might've been as benign as a male classmate popping your bra strap, or smacking you on the behind. And chances are—if you responded with anger—you were told to chill because you were *overreacting*. That's how the seeds are sown. We're taught to shoulder the responsibility of shielding ourselves from harm, and that if someone hurts us, we must examine our actions to figure out why. *Was it something I wore? Was it something I said?*

Which, of course, is bullshit.

Sixty percent of Black girls living in this country have experienced sexual assault before the age of 18. It's not you, sis. It's the world around you. A world that tells people that it's ok to touch you without permission because your skirt was too short, or you drank too much, or you were too *free*. It's patriarchal smoke and mirrors, a nasty parlor trick meant to devalue you. Please don't fall for it.

You deserve better than this world you're inheriting and I'm sorry we couldn't fix it before you had to face this reality. The bad news is that I have no easy answers, the good news is that I am here to give you all the permission you might ever need to not feel ashamed. To not accept any attempts to blame you. To tell the people who try to sell you this lie of culpability in your assault where they can go and how they can get there.

Anyway.

If this has happened to you, I want to tell you right here, right now, that it is not your fault. It is never your fault. And that anger? It's valid. Never feel bad for exercising autonomy over your body. Never apologize for standing your ground, for saying "No," for fighting back. *You* are your strongest advocate, and your fiercest champion. There is nothing to be ashamed of, nothing about you has been dirtied or ruined or whatever other lies might be shoved your way. You survived. That's enough. No one gets to judge you or disrespect you or disregard your pain or your rage.

If this has happened to you, do not hide in shame. Do not be afraid to share your story. Stories are important. They are the thread that connects us. They tell us that we're not alone. Just as you may find solace in these words, someone else may find solace in yours.

With love,

JAMIE

WHAT'S GOOD?

The reason I decided to write this letter is because you might be where I was at 16. When I was 16 years old, I was arrested. I had run away from home because my mother and I were not getting along. I ended up without any money or a place to stay. I came up with the bright idea to rob a taxicab driver at knife point. I was not raised to be violent and I didn't want to do it, but I was desperate. I ended up being arrested and catching felony charges. I spent some time locked up in adult population. Eventually I was released and put on probation.

When I was incarcerated, no one came to see me. All my so-called-friends disappeared, and even family support was limited. There were days I used to stare out of my cell window looking at cars on the highway and wishing I was a passenger going anywhere but where I was. Deep down, I knew I didn't belong in jail. I was smart, talented and creative, but I took responsibility for doing something wrong. The good part is that this moment in my life was not the end of my story.

What do I want you to take from this letter? Know that where you are now does not have to be indicative of where you end up in life. Even during incarceration, you have a choice in how your life shapes up. Make the most of your time by reading, writing and setting goals for the future. Your body may be locked up, but your mind is not. You matter and you have something to offer! Never let anyone tell you that you don't. We all make mistakes in life and we all are worthy of forgiveness and a new page to start over.

I know being positive in this situation is not easy. I know there are days you miss your family and freedom. Some correctional officers will not treat you fairly. There are days you will be filled with rage. You were not put on earth to give in to that anger. You were put here to be a light and vessel of greatness with endless possibilities.

I believe in you! I am rooting for your success and your happiness. Chin up, baby girl! Queens don't let other queens drop their heads or standards. I'll be praying for you!

RENEE

IN SURVIVOR SOLIDARITY,

I'm writing to you from the other side of experiencing sexual violence. I am a Black feminist lesbian incest survivor, child sexual abuse survivor, and young adult rape survivor. When I was ten years old, I was molested for two years by my Pop-pop. I told my parents, but they never addressed it. Around that same time, a family friend rubbed my body without my consent. I was 11ish, and he was 23. I had a big crush on him. I loved receiving special age-appropriate attention from him, but I didn't like it when he touched my body. When I told my father's girlfriend that he had touched my body and also came into the bathroom when I took a shower to beg me not to tell anyone, she immediately told my father who made him move out of our house immediately.

Unfortunately, however, my divorced parents told me that, though the family friend touching my body was wrong, it was my fault because I flirted with him. It wasn't until many years later, when my first therapist told me that, him touching my body wasn't my fault because I was a child, and he was an adult.

I was raped when I was 19 years old in my second year in college when I was on a study abroad program. I broke all the university-enforced rules to go out, very late at night, with the man who would become my rapist. Despite my having second thoughts about going out with this new acquaintance, I was both afraid to articulate them and to turn around because my friends were covering for me (this was in 1989, years before everyone had a cell phone, and before social media existed). We would all get in trouble if I returned after curfew. So, I had to stay out all night until I could sneak back in the morning. In the hotel room, for which I paid, I told my rapist, "I don't want to do this. Please stop." I didn't "violently" fight back. I didn't scream or yell at the top of my lungs because I was afraid. I didn't want to make a "scene." I blamed myself for saying "yes," for breaking the rules, for paying for the hotel room. The morning following my rape, I went back to where the school housed us, and I lied to my friends. I didn't tell them that he forced me to have sex against my will. I had pleasurable, consensual sex with another man less than 24 hours after my rape. For a brief moment in time during that sexual encounter, I denied what happened on the night of my rape. I was also in control of my body again after the rape. When it was time to return home to the United States, I was pregnant. I didn't know which of the two men was the biological father—the rapist or my one-night-stand lover. I was fortunate to have a safe and legal abortion at the former Elizabeth Blackwell Health Center for Women in Philadelphia, PA. I am not a lesbian because I was molested and raped. I am a lesbian because I'm attracted to and love women.

I have not lived your experience and you are not alone. For over 40 years, I have journeyed from a victim of child sexual abuse, other forms of sexual assault, and rape to a survivor of these violations committed against my body without my consent.

Here are a few essential things that I want you to know:

First, if you are underage, and the person who committed sexual harm is an adult or significantly older than you by 3–5 years, you cannot consent to sex even if you really like the person and want to be sexually involved.

Second, if you are sexually active, sexual desire isn't wrong. Rape and other forms of sexual violence are wrong.

Third, you are not a slut, a hoochie, fast, a ho, a whore, a THOT ("that ho over there"), a chickenhead, a sidechick, or any other derogatory word used for Black girls and femmes who are sexually assaulted and raped. You did not get what you deserve. No one deserves to get raped or sexually assaulted. No one. Rape and other forms of sexual violence are vicious forms of terrorism where our bodies are violated and invaded against our will. Regardless of what anyone tells you, you should not be ashamed or blame yourself for the violence committed against your body.

Fourth, sexual violence transcends your gender identity and sexual orientation. It doesn't matter if you are heterosexual or LGBTQI (lesbian, gay, bisexual, transgender, queer, and intersex), any sexual violence you experienced is not your fault.

Fifth, there isn't anything that you can do that results in anyone touching any part of your body against your will. You have the right to say "No." You are allowed to have crushes. You can flirt and even tease. You should have the right to wear what you want. You can kiss and participate in heavy petting, but decide that you don't want to have oral, vaginal, or anal sex. You can participate in oral sex but do not want to have anal sex. You can say, "Yes," to all sexual activity, and change your mind in the middle of the sexual activity.

Sixth, you don't owe anyone sex because they give you special attention, take you out on a date, buy your food, or give you gifts.

Seventh and perhaps most importantly, healing is a long-term journey and never a destination. Please be patient with yourself, and hopefully, you can seek and receive the support you need.

If not, let my words serve as a balm to your wounds, and also as an affirmation of your survivor journey.

In Survivor Solidarity, Always,

AISHAH

—— *Know This* ——

BRYAN STEVENSON is an attorney and activist and the founder of the Equal Justice Initiative. He and his organization have saved 125 men from the death penalty. He also fought in the United States Supreme Court to get the death penalty ruled unconstitutional for children convicted of crimes.

Resources

Dear Sister: Letters to Survivors of Sexual Violence by Lisa Factora Borchers

NO! The Rape Documentary by Aishah Shahidah Simmons/*NO! Study Guide* by Dr. Salamishah Tillet and Rachel Afi Quinn

Hey, Shorty! A Guide to Combating Sexual Harassment and Violence in Schools and on the Streets by Joanne Church, Meghan Huppuch, and Mandy Van Deven

The Sexual Trauma Workbook for Teen Girls: A Guide to Recovery from Sexual Assault and Abuse (Instant Help Books for Teens) by Raychelle Cassada Lohmann, PhD, LPC, and Sheela Raja, PhD

The National Sexual Assault Hotline: (800) 656-4673 (available twenty-four hours a day)

The National Human Trafficking Hotline: (888) 373-7888 or text "HELP" to 233733 (available twenty-four hours a day). (Sexual trafficking means that someone is forcing you to perform sexual acts for money.)

Planned Parenthood provides reproductive healthcare, plus information about your body, relationships, sex, pregnancy, and more. All calls to Planned Parenthood are anonymous, confidential, and free. There are Planned Parenthood centers and hotlines across the country. To find the one nearest you, call (800) 230-PLAN.

LETTER TO MY BLACK GIRL SELF

Sometimes when we feel guilt, we isolate ourselves. We hide our scars and traumas from view. We hide what we think is "wrongness." We feel alone. Write a letter about a tough thing that you are facing or have faced. It's okay; you don't have to show it to anybody. Naming our feelings is the first step to healing ourselves.

CHAPTER 6

BLACK GIRL, INTERRUPTED

Mental Health

IT'S NOT CRAZY

There is more than one sort of "health." We are often encouraged to take care of our bodies—to eat well, exercise, and rest. Most of us wouldn't hesitate to tell someone if we didn't feel physically well. We would visit a doctor if we were faced with a serious physical injury—if we broke a leg or developed a very high fever. We know our physical health is important. In some cases, we cannot *live* without it. Black girl, I want you to be just as vigilant about your mental health—most people are not.

The tweens and teens can be a difficult time for you. Your body is changing. You have more responsibilities. So much is happening. A lot of girls experience an increase in depression in their early teen years. But for many Black girls, that depression never leaves. In a study by the African American Policy Forum, 67 percent of Black girls said they had felt sad or hopeless for two or more weeks straight. Maybe instead of depressed, you feel anxious. Or maybe something in your head just doesn't feel right and you can't explain. Learn to pay as much attention to these illnesses as you would a fever or a broken bone. Just like physical illness, mental illness can be managed. Just like physical illness, untreated mental illness can interrupt your future.

Because of fixed, negative ideas about Black girls, people often forget that you need emotional support. They think you have everything handled. And then, there is "attitude." Biased people often mistake a Black girl's cry for help as just her being hard to deal with. This happens to Black women, too. But know this today, Black girl—there is no shame in making your mental health a priority and the people around you owe you their support.

In the letters that follow, Black women share their stories of overcoming emotional distress and remind you that your mental health matters.

Hey There, Lovely

I want to tell you a story about myself, what I was going through when I was around your age.

I went through a rough time in my teenage days. At school, the group I thought were my best friends all turned on me and I went from having a crew to not knowing where to eat lunch or who to sit next to anymore. It was the worst.

At home, my parents were fighting a lot. Infidelity almost broke up their marriage. I knew too much, too early. More than I wanted to know. I felt like I had to choose sides between my mom and dad. It was tough.

Besides that, I wasn't good at most subjects and couldn't imagine a future for myself. I compared myself to others and felt so much less than them—less pretty, less cool, less intelligent, less everything. I was shouldering a lot of heavy burdens all at the same time.

Even though I was dealing with all those things, I was supposed to somehow keep it together and be strong and get through it and still get good grades. But I remember being angry and sad and feeling powerless. My grades went down. I started making bad decisions about food, and my parents couldn't understand that I was developing an eating disorder. They didn't know how to help me, so I got quite a few tough talks and a frustrated attitude instead of the kind of understanding I needed. My parents are old school. Maybe you know how that goes too.

So I wound up going to the guidance counselor's office. Her name was Dr. Pierre. And Dr. Pierre's office turned out to be the best place for me.

It was a safe place away from all my sources of stress, where I could talk out my feelings about everything I was dealing with. It was a place to make plans for my future.

On Sunday I would go with my family to church and pray. During the week, after class I could go to the counselor's office to lay my burdens down. She never gave me the answers. I used to get so annoyed, just like "tell me what to do!" But she never would. Instead she would let me talk things out and find the answers for myself. Every now and then she would ask a question like "how do you feel about that?"

It was my first introduction to therapy. It's how I first was able to recognize that my issues were deeper than just being sad or going through hard times or being a teenager, whatever that means. It was the first time I understood what my depression and anxiety looked like. It helped me begin to cope with all the stuff that was weighing me down, it helped me realize that I couldn't control what I was experiencing but I could try to control my reactions. I honestly think I would have been lost and could have made some monumentally bad life decisions if I hadn't spent as much time as I did, in that office, confronting what I was dealing with and figuring out my feelings.

I want you to know it's OK to seek help. It's important to find your own safe space where you can lay your burdens down.

I want you to know that going to a psychiatrist, therapist or counselor doesn't make you weak. It doesn't mean you're broken. It doesn't mean you're crazy. It means you're strong enough to recognize that you could use some perspective.

I want you to know that it's often necessary to confront your pain, even when it may be more convenient to ignore it. You gotta deal with it to get past it, most of the time.

I want you to know this is coming from a place of understanding. Know that you aren't alone. Know that trouble doesn't last always. Know that it can and truly will get better if you keep holding on and do what you need to do, to heal and grow.

I get it. I feel you. I love you.

PATRICE
(But some call me Afrobella)

···

Dear Black Girl,

You are facing a world that does not always value you; a world that expects you to be strong; a world that wants you to embrace your girlhood and innocence, but also take on adult responsibilities. People may expect you to just "handle it" if someone tries to steal your Black Girl Joy or uses your developing curves as a justification for assault. The crushing pressure, anger, and frustration that can be a part of Black girlhood can feel overwhelming.

Black girl, you are allowed to feel overwhelmed and to expect that there will be others who will take away some of the burden. You are permitted to feel sad, frustrated, anxious—and to have those feelings acknowledged.

If you hear that there is no space for your expression of feelings, no resources to provide you support, or that Black girls don't struggle, do not believe this. Your emotional wellness matters, because YOU matter. Your feelings—they are real.

Your trauma over things that have happened to you is real.

Your worry about encountering racism or other poor treatment is real.

Your anxiety or depression are real—even if you cannot quite figure what causes them.

Your anger—that others call "attitude"—is real.

Your hopelessness when it feels your community does not value or see you—or that it values Black boys over you—is real.

The first step in making your emotional health important is making it okay to say that you experience all these things. They are REAL.

The unfairness in our society, especially the sexism and racism directed at Black girls, can cause and reinforce fear, loneliness and self-doubt. I work with lots of girls like you and I know that what some folks call "attitude" or being "difficult" is your expression of how hard it is to be you—Black and girl—in spaces that do not seem to care about either identity.

Black girl, you do not have to be strong all the time. You *do* have to care about yourself all the time. As you grow and become a woman, find spaces and people who will help you navigate your journey in all its beauty, awkwardness, and pain. Demand spaces where you can be vulnerable and express—without fear of getting in trouble or being ignored—your worries, your hopes and your doubts. You do not—should not—have to figure this out alone. There is no shame in seeing a therapist if you need to. We go to doctors to keep our bodies healthy; we can go to doctors to keep our minds healthy, too. It is also important to have *Black girl* spaces, where you can be honest and real with people who understand your experience best. Do not let anyone, even Black women, tell you that your problems are not important, that you should be stronger. (Sadly, many of us received these bad messages when we were girls. We still receive them. We are just repeating what we know.)

When you have people, who support you without judgement; when you have circles of supportive black girls and women; when you have therapy to heal your mind; hopefully you will come to know that you deserve joy. Not simple happiness—but *joy*. Joy is having access to people, places and activities that speak to your soul, soothe your spirit, bring you hope and make your heart soar.

It is not enough for Black girls like us to just know about our pain or to speak on it. We must also allow ourselves the time and resources to move toward good emotional health. We have to have space to heal. People may not offer us this space willingly, but, Black girl, know you are worthy of it. As you move into womanhood, *take* your space.

Go in Joy.

TYFFANI

HEY SISTER,

I don't even know what to call this. Do I call it a love letter? A think piece? A call to action?

No. See, none of these fit. This isn't about eloquent thoughts, or demands for you to do more than what you've already done for this world. This is my body talking to yours. My spirit, to yours.

Seems like only during periods of grief, do our hearts get to meet in such a vulnerable way. Seems like we only get seen for our softness when the world exposes its deep brokenness. I'm sorry. We both deserve better.

I'd love to know your heart outside of turmoil, I'd love to know its softness. What a heavy load we carry, sister; birthing nations, cultivating cultures, and raising both what this country will call "legends" and "thugs" depending on how fast they dribble. Then we watch in rage as all three get ripped from our wombs and placed at the mercy of a system that will deny you credit of all but the one they reject. I'm not naive to how impossible it feels to be both hard and soft, both strong and collapsible.

How impossible it seems to feel fully and shamelessly, yet still be expected to show up and do. But still, we carry that load—gracefully and gently. We rise softly to embrace and guide our babies (young and old) who are afraid. We use our soft bodies as shields between batons and the bodies of Black men. We use our breast and soft brain matter to nurse an unforgiving country.

What a heavy load, what a lot to do.

I see your softness today, sister. And I honor it. I've been forced to sit in mine so deeply these past few weeks. I've wept and crumbled in ways that felt foreign, but familiar and necessary. I honor it. Because I know it's not just my pain, but yours too. Our mommas, and aunties and grandmas.

I've wanted to do, teach, and fight so much recently, but my spirit has other plans. She's asked me to sit still in my softness and begin healing.

As a therapist for Black women, as a healer, I've been tasked with the questions of the heart. The questions of the spirit. And let me tell you, sister, the answers don't come with to-do lists.

So, you know, maybe this is an "ask piece." Can I ask you to sit in your softness too? To allow the grief of countless generations to move through your body, allow it to unravel you and escape into tears and ruthless self-care, culminating in stillness.

Can I ask you to fight the urge to sew it back up into a neat package, or a list of action items? Can we take advantage of the emotional rawness bubbling up, hold it, nurture it, and let it dissolve into the earth instead of adding it to our load to unpack later? Or for our children to unpack?

I believe it's time for us to rest, sister. Can I ask you to BE, today, instead of do? That is quite revolutionary, too. Rest.

Let us not only be the generation that showed up in the streets and demanded justice, but let us be the generation that took time to heal. We know too well what it looks like when that isn't prioritized.

I wish rest for you, free of shame. I wish healing for you, free of duty. I wish us peace and will be here to continuously remind you that you deserve it.

I love you.

Yours,

IEASHA

— *Know This* —

Resources

Twenty-four-hour Crisis Text Line: Text 741741 from anywhere in the US and you will receive an automated text asking you what your crisis is. Within minutes, a live trained crisis counselor will answer your text. The text exchange is free, is confidential, and will not appear on your phone statement.

National Suicide Prevention Lifeline: (800) 273-8255. Option for deaf and hard of hearing: (800) 799-4889.

The Trevor Project (*TheTrevorProject.org*) is the leading national organization providing crisis intervention and suicide prevention services to lesbian, gay, bisexual, transgender, queer, and questioning (LGBTQ) young people under twenty-five.

TeenMentalHealth.org

You Got This! A Girl's Guide to Growing Up by Dr. Tyffani Monford Dent

Girls Got Issues: A Woman's Guide to Self-discovery and Healing by Dr. Tyffani Monford Dent

According to Dr. Tyffani Monford Dent, common signs of anxiety include

- Negative thoughts
- Trouble sleeping

- Feeling panicky, scared, or worried
- Physical symptoms such as a racing heart, shaking, and dizziness; also stomach upset, including pain
- Obsessing over physical symptoms

According to *HelpGuide.org*, common signs of depression include

- Constantly feeling irritable, sad, or angry
- Not finding fun in activities you used to love
- Feeling worthless and bad about yourself
- Sleeping too much or not enough
- Using alcohol or drugs to try to change the way you feel
- Having frequent, unexplained headaches or other physical pains or problems
- Crying easily; extreme sensitivity
- Gaining or losing weight without trying to
- Having trouble concentrating, remembering things, or focusing on schoolwork
- Thinking about death or suicide (if you feel like you might hurt yourself, please tell someone or call the hotline number listed earlier)

Letter to My Black Girl Self

How do you feel, Black girl? We aren't always encouraged to be in touch with our feelings. Write a letter about how you feel right now. Be as specific as you can. It is perfectly normal to feel more than one thing at a time. For instance, you can be excited about hanging out with a new boo, but kind of nervous, too. Be sure to read what you have written. Ask yourself: Are your feelings something you should share with another trusted person? Are you feeling fine or do you need help?

CHAPTER 7

BOO'D UP

Sex

S-E-X

The whole sex thing is weird, right? It's everywhere. Megan Thee Stallion is rapping about it. Boys and girls in high school are texting about it. It's in movies and on TV. Booties are hanging out all over social media. Everybody is concerned with being sexy—pouting in the camera and working their angles. Everybody wants to talk about sex, but nobody really wants to *talk* about sex, which is this big deal thing that can be fun, yes, but also has the power to change a girl's life permanently.

Nobody wants to talk much about *not* being ready for sex. Nobody wants to talk much about double standards—how it is so easy for Black girls to be shamed for sexual feelings, while boys get cheers. Nobody wants to talk much about protection if you aren't in health class. Nobody wants to talk much about pleasure—how a girl learns what she likes. Nobody wants to talk much about what to do if you are a queer kid and everybody leaves you out of the conversation. What does *your* safe sex even look like? Why won't anyone talk about that?

It is all so complicated—more so because of those fixed negative views about Black girls. Folks act like you already know too much about sex. They act like your body is an invitation. They don't remind you that there is no shame in sexual desire or being curious about pleasure, because they think you are already shameless. Meanwhile, you are just trying to figure it all out.

In the letter that follows, a Black woman shares the important things she taught her Black girl about S-E-X.

....

DEAR BLACK GIRL,

The auntie who wants to talk to you about . . . sex? Yeah, that's me.

To be honest with you, it isn't more fun for me to talk about this stuff than it is for you to listen to it. The difference is, I know how important it is. I know you believe that you have it figured out or that you have time to learn. I'm telling you that is so true in some ways and yet also the most untrue thing you've ever believed.

Let's start here: Sex isn't a bad thing. You don't have to run from it. You don't have to be ashamed of having sexual urges. You don't have to be afraid. Adults try to make you afraid of sex and your sexual being in the hopes that it'll keep you from exploring, and thus, making potential mistakes. But guess what? No matter how old and experienced you are, you're still going to make mistakes in that arena. There's no way around it. Relationships—romantic, sexual, and otherwise—are fraught with potholes. There are numerous ways to slip up or fall. You're human. You will hurt and be hurt. Learn to forgive yourself first and let that compassion for yourself cause you to extend it in equal measure to others.

When I was about your age, I decided that if and when I had my own daughter, I would be different with her than my mother was with me when it came to discussions around sex. I would be open, honest, happy to communicate and have the hard conversations. I did have a daughter, Sarai, who at the time I'm writing this is almost 17. According to her, I have never made her feel that she couldn't talk to me, so I think I've done a pretty good job so far. At 5, this kid asked me how babies got out of a mommy's tummy. At 6, she asked me how babies got in (yes, I explained sex to a six-year-old). At 7, we had a full-blown conversation about birth control options over her birthday dinner at the Cheesecake Factory. There have been times when I've embarrassed the hell out of her, I'm sure, but I'm the reason why, when a friend told her that she was ready to have sex, Sarai walked with her to the nearest drugstore and showed her where the condoms were.

If your mom or real-life aunties haven't had those embarrassing necessary conversations with you, allow me to butt in, just a little bit.

Coming into your sexual personhood happens in a different way for everyone. You don't have to be ready to have sex at 16. You don't have to be ready to have sex ever (asexual people exist). Allow yourself the freedom to explore slowly. You have a lifetime of finding out what you like and that's a big part of the fun.

Make safer sex a requirement. Especially when you're young. Preventing unwanted pregnancy and the spread of infection are important. Learn about condoms and dental dams.

There is no shame in abortion and it isn't a sin. Your body belongs to you alone and you have the wherewithal to make choices that are right for you. No loving god will smite you for choosing yourself.

Sex isn't something that is done to you. Sex is an experience to share with your partners. It should be pleasurable for all involved. If the person you're having sex with shows no interest in your pleasure or your instructions to help you reach orgasm and have a fun experience, that person isn't worthy of you, your body, your energy, or your time.

Be vocal. Tell your partner what feels good to you and makes you comfortable. You deserve nothing but pleasant experiences.

Masturbation is good. You can't tell someone how to touch you if you don't know how you like to be touched. Also . . . there's no safer sex than sex with yourself, love.

Your body is beautiful. YOU are beautiful. Make sure you know that so you aren't depending on any romantic partner to make you feel good in your own skin.

If you are queer, that is good and normal and natural. You aren't the only one. You're not alone. There's nothing wrong with you.

Make "no" your favorite word. Understand the need for boundaries. Set them early and often and hold them without fail.

Sex isn't the technicalities. It isn't just the body movements. And honey, it isn't anything you've seen in those clips on your phone. It is messier, more awkward, and way more fun than you can imagine— when it's done right and with those who make you feel at home with their bodies and yours. Give yourself time to find those people. Give yourself time to become one of those people. There's no rush.

And if you have a question you can't ask your mama, come find me. I'll take you out for cheesecake.

All my love,

TITI

——*Know This*——

Resources

Changing Bodies, Changing Lives by Ruth Bell

Body Drama by Nancy Amanda Redd

Planned Parenthood (*PlannedParenthood.org/Learn/Teens*)

Scarleteen: Sex Ed for the Real World (*Scarleteen.com*)

LGBTCenters.org: Directory of nationwide centers for the LGBTQ community

Letter to Your Black Girl Self

Coming into your sexual personhood happens in a different way for everyone. You don't have to be ready to have sex now or ever. You may want to engage in sexual intimacy one day. Write a letter to yourself about what you think it means to be "ready" for sexual activity. What do you think you need to know about your body? About a potential partner? What might you need to protect yourself? Be specific.

CHAPTER 8

GIRL, LISTEN . . .

Advice

YOU FIRST

For Black folks like us, family and community are important. We *have* to care for and look out for each other. But learn this today and learn it well: You cannot give if you have nothing. You cannot help an anxious friend if you are about to break. You can't teach if you haven't learned. You can't have a happy, healthy relationship with Bae if you don't pay attention to what makes *you* happy. Those fixed, negative ideas about Black girls and women say that our needs don't matter all that much; we should focus on being pleasing and helpful to other people. But, girl, you've got to love and take care of yourself first and foremost. Without your health, well-being, and stability, you can't be a blessing to your family, your community, or your friends.

In the final letters of *Dear Black Girl*, Black women give you an invaluable gift—they explain what actively loving yourself as a Black girl looks like. They define self-care. Now, you may have heard these words associated with manicures, massages, and vacations. And those things can be ways to treat yourself if you have the ability. But that's not the most nourishing way to put yourself first. *Real* self-care looks like owning your name—even if it's a Blackity Black name and other people can't pronounce it or think that it is weird. It means honoring your ideas and Black girl creativity. It looks like making decisions that support your health, happiness, and future goals. It looks like learning how to advocate for your needs in the most successful way possible. It looks like surrounding yourself with good friends, especially Black girls and women who support and love you no matter what. It looks like setting boundaries and protecting them. It looks like acting selfishly to live selflessly. It looks like remembering Black girl joy.

There is more advice in the pages to come. But, Black girl, know this: whatever you want out of life for you and the people and community that surround you, you have to love yourself enough to know you deserve it and you have to love yourself *first* to achieve it.

DEAR BEAUTIFUL BLACK GIRL,

I've been thinking about my younger years and how I got to where I am. At 33, there are so many things I am still learning about myself and life. (Heads up: Life is a never-ending process. Seriously!) But I am going to share with you some things that I needed to hear at your age: You really can grow up to do and be anything you want to be, but you have to hustle.

That idea that you have been thinking back and forth about? Make sure you do something with it as soon as possible. You were given that idea for a reason and the world deserves to experience your brilliance.

Your body is yours and yours alone. As the reigning goddess of your temple, be brave enough to walk away from anyone who does not acknowledge your boundaries. "No" is a complete sentence—no matter how cute or how charming he, she or they may be. And protect your health at all costs.

Your adult life will most likely be different from what you imagine. The woman you will become will be shaped by a rapidly changing world. The best part about all of it is that as you grow, you will adapt, which is a very important life skill. The life you end up with in 5, 10 or even 20 years can be much deeper than you can imagine at your current age. Let this excite you, not scare you, and move accordingly.

Lastly, if you happen to have an "ethnic" name like I do, do not trust anyone who insists on shortening or altering it in favor of something more palatable. You were given that name. It has been one of the first things to shape your life. Make them say it—full out. Who you are is non-negotiable!

I am sure that at some point you have learned how hard it is to be a Black girl in a white man's world. But you have so many big sisters, aunties and mamas in this world that will support you. We are waiting for you.

You are amazing.

You are worthy of all the things.

You are brilliant.

You are valuable.

The world should see you shine.

Cheering you on, little sis,

FOLASHADE

DEAR BLACK GIRL,

I am writing this letter to share that in all your doing, achieving, living, learning and loving of others, please make a promise first to LOVE YOU SOME YOU! You live in a world that won't always see how great you are—even if it sees it, the world won't always want to acknowledge it.

Your inner beauty and power will feel like a threat to some people *especially* if you make loving yourself important. Those people will try to convince you (often in subtle ways) that you should take a back seat to those they feel are more entitled to great things in life. Girls with blonde hair and blue eyes. Girls at nicer schools. Girls who are thinner or who have the "right" shape—tiny waists, big booties and thick thighs. Girls with lots of money and fancy friends. Some people will not hesitate to say that because you may not have some of this or other things they think matter, you should take a back seat.

When you feel this, beautiful Black girl, reinforce your armor by taking care of yourself first and foremost. Here is how:

Recognize that you are Beauty Personified. You are the offspring of millions of beautiful Black women. There are countless famous examples: Serena Williams, Alicia Keys, Phylicia Rashad, Nicki Minaj, Angela Rye, Harriet Tubman, Lupita Nyong'o, Barbara Jordan, H.E.R. More importantly, you can spot this beauty just by walking out of your door and looking around your neighborhood and school. There is beauty in the Black woman who is caring for her children with little or no help and the bold beautiful Black woman cashier at the neighborhood Walmart. Only beauty comes from beauty. Facts! Recognize these women as a mirror reflection of your own beauty, as your beauty is a reflection of them.

Feed your mind the best food. Read the works of great Black writers, like Toni Morrison, Alice Walker, J. California Cooper, Zora Neale Hurston, Octavia Butler and Paule Marshall. Read the literary classics. Read! Read! Read!

Feed your body the best food and drink you can. Drinking loads of water, eating those veggies, lean protein and indulging your sweet tooth only sometimes goes a long way. I know it isn't easy. Sometimes eating something that tastes good can make you feel better. Sometimes our neighborhoods don't always have groceries stores with good food—the bodega or corner store may only carry a few, janky-looking apples. Maybe your family can't always afford the fresh stuff. Just do your best. Also, exercise. I don't care what it is—walk, dance, turn cartwheels. Just move and keep moving. This is where I have struggled the most—eating right and moving—but I know that when I'm on top of this, I feel on top of the world!

Nothing redeeming can come from smoking, doing drugs or excessive drinking. You want every inch of your beauty to show up regularly. Trust me, you won't find any value in anything that will diminish that.

Keep company with the most encouraging friends and associates. Surround yourself with like-minded people who show up for you and encourage you and allow you to do the same for them. Be among those who have dreams and goals because these people will help to fuel your dreams and desires. And find mentors—people who have proven that dreams can come true even if obstacles crop up and are willing to share that wisdom with you.

Educate yourself about the world you want to live in and the work that you want to do in it. In addition to learning about your own beautiful Black culture, don't hesitate to learn about other cultures, especially the cultures of people who have had to overcome obstacles as our people have. Learn about foods, rituals, languages and how others celebrate life. And travel, too!

Once you've recognized what your gifts and talents are, throw your whole self into them with love and every drop of passion you have! If you attend college or some specialized program, learn your major course of study inside and out so that you can bring your highest self to the world that you will be serving. This, I guarantee you, will bring you joy and fulfillment.

This is what it means to love you some you. Love yourself first and that leads to a genuine love of others.

May you reach your highest ground,

ROBIN

Dearest,

There is something in us Black girls. We can imagine a whole wide, brilliant, beautiful world before we even open our eyes in the morning and every breath we take gets us closer to it. As you dream and breathe and love and grow, you carry not only yourself, but all us Black girls with you. And you know that means as I breathe and love and grow, I carry you with me. And the Black girls from before me and after you? They carry us, too. We are everlasting.

I want you to know that there are many hard things in this world. There is pain and loss and poverty and we Black girls know it better than most. But guess what we also know? We know that there is no shame in asking for help. We know that the communities we build make us stronger and help us carry pain. We know that for there to be loss, there has to be joy and love. And, oh, do we feel joy and love! Our joy and love has brought empires to their knees. The music and art and poetry we create from our too full hearts has spread that joy and love and helped the whole world grieve and grow from loss. Our spirit—yours, mine and the spirits of all the Black girls—our spirits fight and win. We see poverty and injustice and we fight it smarter and harder than anyone else. You've heard that Black girls are magic? It's true. You are magic carried in a great current of spells and prayers.

One last thing, dear—being yourself, listening to your intuition and following your heart are the bravest and most magical things you can do on this earth. A lot of expectations are placed on Black girls, but you do not owe anyone anything. Your only responsibility is to be true to yourself. All that Black girl magic lies deep inside you and every day when you open your eyes, all you have to do is listen for that magic.

Trust yourself and you'll join all the other Black girls building a brilliant, beautiful world.

We love you and we need you, always.

SARAH

. . . .

DEAR EMERGENT YOUNG BLACK WOMAN,

The most important piece of advice that I would give you is this: Develop an unshakeable and nonnegotiable belief in your own worth. This one thing has kept me going in my darkest hours.

Define yourself by your own boundless terms and never anyone else's paltry caricature of you. You are enough exactly as you are and any flaws you think you have or mistakes you think you've made are nothing more than evidence of your wild, quirky, glorious humanity. None of it dulls your shine or makes you any less valuable.

Because you are so valuable, do not feel obligated to let everyone into your circle. Your time, energy, resources and spirit belong to you and they are worthy of your protection. It is good that you are loving, good and open your heart to others. The gifts you share bring your unique light into the world. Always remember, though, that you have every right to set boundaries in defense of your own wellbeing. You set the terms on which you give your gifts. Never let anyone make you feel badly for choosing who and what you allow into your mind and your life.

Lastly, learn to take care of your valuable self. You'll have to define what self-care means to you, but I have a few suggestions. Make time to be in the places and with the people who feed your soul. Seek knowledge and develop wisdom. Practice a hobby (or several) for the sheer joy of it and learn new skills. Find exercise you enjoy. Get enough sleep and prioritize your health. Eat foods that make your body feel good and wear whatever clothes make you feel at home in your skin. Develop a balance between serving others and taking time to recharge. Learn to disengage gracefully from things that take too much from you for too little reward. Sometimes the world pressures women—especially Black ones—to give without expecting to receive;

to care for others without expecting to be cared for ourselves. You can't fill anything or anyone from an empty vessel; keep yourself full, too!

That's all for now, dear one. I hope these few bits of advice from someone who has been there before will resonate with you and that you will find some of it useful and encouraging for your journey. The road may not always be easy, but equip yourself well and travel in confidence.

You got this!

I wish you all the best in life.

Yours truly,

TWILA

....

DEAR HOPE,

I call you hope because I believe in you. You are my hope for the future.

I've started this letter in my head dozens of times and I keep coming back to one main point: Love yourself. Everything else—how you show up in the world, your relationships with other people and your resilience; your ability to come back from disappointment, heartache, cruelty and failure—all of these things will be built on the foundation of your self-love and self-respect.

Looking back, I was extremely blessed in my upbringing. I had my mom, dad and grandmother in the home to raise me and my two older siblings. My parents worked hard and we had everything we needed (although not everything we wanted). We were disciplined and there were high expectations for our behavior and achievement. I think the worst thing in the world for me—my greatest fear—would be to disappoint my parents.

My dad had a way of turning that fear of disappointment around on us. As we became teenagers, he told us that we should act selfishly. He said if we acted selfishly, he'd never really have to worry about us.

Well, that seemed to be the craziest thing I had ever heard. He couldn't mean that. There were a whole lot of things I wanted to do or try that selfishly might make me happy—things I knew he would hate! What if I wanted to use his car and stay out late? What if I wanted to cheat on a test so that I would get a better grade? What if I wanted to take something I wanted, even though it didn't belong to me? Selfish? Yeah, right.

But Daddy was playing the long game. When he talked about acting selfishly, he did it in a way to make us think about long-term consequences. If I chose behavior that would put me at risk, like stealing or staying out late or cheating—that was stupid, not selfish. If I wanted to engage in risky behavior to be around a cute boy, I needed to think about what the best thing for me would be. And if I made choices that would earn my parents' disapproval, I needed to think it through and approach those choices in ways that would work best for me—FOR ME—not my friends, not my siblings and not even my parents. I had to love myself enough to make good decisions and to trust in them.

Trusting yourself is a big hairy deal. Here is what trusting yourself does not mean: You will always make the right decision. No one makes the right decision all the time. In fact, sometimes we make a series of wrong decisions and then we beat ourselves up for being so dumb. Staying in a cycle of regret over a bad choice helps nothing. LEARNING from a mistake builds strength. There's a saying: "We learn wisdom from failure much more than success." Not that failure doesn't suck sometimes. But since it is inevitable, good to know there's an upside to it.

I need you to trust in your ability to survive. Trust in your ability to grow and get past disappointment and hurt. Trust yourself to know that even when you get knocked down, there's still a way to climb back up.

My high school boyfriend and I went to the same college. Terrible mistake. We needed time to mature and grow separate from each other. When we broke up, it was all drama. Ugly. I let my emotions rule everything and I did and said things for which I am ashamed. Once I got back home and faced my dad, he said, "My biggest disappointment is that you didn't act with self-respect. You lost your pride." That was another way of saying I had failed to act selfishly.

I said, "But, Daddy, aren't there times when love is more important than pride?"

His response was immediate. "Damn few. Damn few. If your mother came in here tomorrow and told me she was leaving, I'd ask her some questions, but I'd never try to stop her. She has to respect me and I have to respect her." (By the way—my parents were married 55 years.)

He was telling me that rejection, whether by a person or a job or a group or a school or anyone, could not define me. I define me. I have to love myself enough to know who I am.

I also had to learn the meaning of "NMS." That stands for Not My, uh, Stuff. (You can substitute another word if you want.) NMS is the awareness that everyone has multiple things going on in their lives at the same time. When your best friend suddenly has attitude towards you, it may have nothing to do with you and everything to do with a bad situation at home or someone who has done something bad to them. It's always better to be a stand-up, loyal friend and offer support. Ride or die. But not really, 'cause if you die, you can't be around to help the next time. See—act selfishly. Setting boundaries can actually be a selfless act. Learn when to walk away. Your selfishness can put you in a better situation to support those you love.

Once you wrap your mind around a commitment to selfishness and self-love, you recognize what a gift it is to share parts of yourself with others. Maybe it's volunteering. Maybe it's your kindness. Maybe it's just your presence, silently offering support and helping another person know that they should love themselves, too. Selfishness does not require insults or making other people feel bad.

Love the body you've been given. Treat it well and don't let others talk you into mistreatment, whether at your own hand or someone else's. Be mindful about what you put into your body. This is where the selfish part can get really tricky. Too much food, or the wrong foods, can be selfishly delicious. Alcohol and weed can feel great, until they don't. The touch of a certain person can feel like heaven. Within boundaries. You have the ability to make your body feel wonderful. Respect that power.

I was almost 50 years old before I started to incorporate regular exercise into my life. Dumb, huh? My mother was an extremely attractive woman—movie star beautiful. I was a chubby teen. She tried to encourage me to diet. It felt like she wanted to change me, because I disappointed her. The thing is, now I love how it feels to work my muscles and stay fit. I love the sense of self-awareness it gives me about how I show up in the world. It is beautiful I am beautiful. I didn't know that for a long, long time. I know now. And when people compliment me, it's an affirmation of what I already know. I define me.

Love yourself enough to take chances. Find your passion. Know that it may be a series of tries and failures to figure it out and know that your passions may change a number of times. Exploring your gifts and your passions may lead you to sharing those gifts—a ripple effect that can spread joy.

Respect your mind. Feed it. Read. Read. Read. Read books, long articles and learn from other perspectives. Listen to music. Play music. Perform music. Dance. See plays. Write for yourself; write things that won't be shared by text or on social media. View art. Define new art. Create art and beauty—even if you are the only audience.

Learn how to be still—to sit with your thoughts. Respect them. Believe that it can be better to be alone than to be with a person or people who do not recognize the value of your company. Even if they do, understand the value of spending time alone with yourself. See yourself as your best company.

Respect yourself. Love yourself. Know that you are worthy of love and respect.

I love you.

LYNNE

. . . .

HEY BLACK GIRL!

Did you know there is a divine cord that binds us together? We cannot be separated. Our strength is in our stories. The stories of our ancestors, who overcame the unthinkable, were kept from us, yet their stories linger in our spirit. We are here because they were. They were the ones who survived. Appreciate and welcome what unites us.

Hey Black girl, sometimes you will be called unworthy and treated unfairly, just because of the color of your skin. Remember you are the most stunning being God created. You wear his thumbprint.

Hey Black girl, sometimes your femininity will be dishonored. You will be told you are weak because of it. Remember you are the backbone of our race. Remember you are resilient. You are a builder where innovation and creativity thrive.

Hey Black girl, do you know how powerful you truly are? You can do anything you put your mind to. You can achieve the unachievable. You can conceive the inconceivable. You can overcome the impossible. You are a force. Every day remember who you are and the reason you live.

I wish when I was growing up there were Black women to remind me of how great I was and why I had to be serious about living to my full potential. Not just for myself but for those little Black girls who were looking at me, ready to mimic what they saw me do.

I wish when I was growing up there were Black women, besides my mom, to encourage me to live my best every day.

I wish when I was growing up there were Black women, strangers, to greet me with love and wisdom whenever they could.

If only I'd had Black women like that take an interest in me. Would I be in a different place? That I'll never know. No time to regret what didn't happen. Cause now, I am 66 years old, doin' what I can while I can. I accept the chance to be one of those Black women. It's my turn to be who I wish I had when I was a little Black girl growing up. That is why I write this letter to you.

Hey Black girl, never doubt yourself. Listen to that inner voice, your conscience, that tells you right from wrong.

Hey Black Girl, always know you are loved and admired. I am proud of you and the woman you will become.

Hey Black Girl, walk upright, shoulders back and head up. Dress in a way so the world knows that you know, you are the daughter of the Queens who birthed you and the Grandmothers who laid bread-crumbs for you to follow to your greatness. Set your sights high and believe in yourself. You are the keeper of what makes us phenomenal ... our Blackness.

Hey Black Girl, don't listen to people who tell you, "You can't."

Don't listen to people who tell you, "You ain't pretty."

Don't listen to people who tell you, "You ain't smart." No, don't drink the Kool-Aid.

Black Girl, you represent the future of Black Power, Black Culture, Black Love.

Deep inside, those people know "YOU CAN, YOU ARE MORE THAN CUTE AND YOU ARE INTELLIGENT!" Pray for them. They need help, not you. You stay true to you.

Wear that responsibility proudly because I and Black women like me are here for you.

Respectfully, stand on our shoulders and not our backs.

Black Girl, you can reach the sky! It's yours for the taking.

From my heart to your mind,

DADA MKUBWA DIXON (BIG SISTER DIXON)

DEAR BLACK GIRL,

Never Stop Playing! Seriously, never stop playing as you did when you were 10, 5, 3 years old.

Be aware that everything you need to know about adulthood, you actually learned in pre-school. Take naps, be kind, eat balanced meals, wash your hands, and play.

Remember the joy of being a kindergartner and playing games with your classmates? Have you ever put on an un-brushed, tattered wig and fiercely whipped your head around as if you're Beyoncé, or at least one of her back-up dancers? Fun, and joy.

Playing is fun. In your early-learning years, there was probably a room or an area in your home dedicated to play. Your guardians understood the importance of play for your development.

Playing creates joy. It is vital for you to find a way to play—for the rest of your life. Look at "play" as a tool for survival and a means of self-care. As you glide into adulthood, you must create time and space in your life to continuously do the things that you love.

I'm telling you to keep doing the things that take your mind off of school, money and anything that weighs heavy on you. Making time and space for play, artistic expression and creativity is like taking a mini-vacation from your regularly scheduled grind. It is therapeutic.

Think of your playtime as a safe-room for your sanity. A metaphorical place in your life where you can go to relax, exhale deeply and reconnect with your authentic self. Allow yourself an occasional excursion into your "playroom" to clear your mind.

Let your artist, your wild dancer, your loud singer or simply "Little Girl You" run free without judgment or boundaries. Take time to charge up your battery with play so you'll have the energy and strength you need for the challenges you'll face.

I must say, some folks are more comfortable with the word "hobbies" or "me-time" or maybe "leisure activities" rather than "play." That's fine, it's the same thing. I like to use the word play because, simply, it sounds more fun.

The idea of a grown woman "at play" may sound radical to put it nicely, or weird if we're not mincing words around here. Truth be told, I've been a "radical weirdo" since high school—with no deference to folks who laughed towards me or raised a curious brow. Regular retreats to my creative "play space" over a lifetime have made me the unbothered, self-assured Free Woman that I am today.

As you work hard to complete high school, then graduate from college or trade school and start a career, circumstances of life will constantly try to separate the overwhelmed, overburdened version of yourself from the joyful, confident carefree you. Don't ever get too far away from your joy! Your joy will always be your pain's favorite sister.

Even if you become president of a nation, be sure to have a room dedicated to practicing your feed-in braids and making friendship bracelets. Never get too far away from who you are today.

Never forget how to play.

Love,

MARY

—*Know This*—

BLACK GIRLS ROCK! is an exciting annual awards show that showcases Black girls and women doing great things. Watch *BlackGirlsRock.com* for ongoing opportunities for learning, growth, and wellness.

MEDITATION is training yourself to be aware and to watch your thoughts and feelings without judgement and with a calm and clear mind. You can start meditating by sitting comfortably in a quiet space; set a timer for three minutes; and begin taking steady breaths, counting each one (inhale . . . exhale . . . 1 . . . inhale . . . exhale . . . 2). When you get to 10, start over again. If your mind wanders, simply bring it back and start over counting. Pay attention to how you feel when your meditation is over. Are you calmer? More relaxed? Try this each morning or in the evening before going to bed.

RADICAL SELF-CARE means prioritizing your physical and mental well-being above all else. You cannot pour your love and support into others if your own cup is empty. Our amazing foremother, activist and writer Audre Lorde said, "Caring for myself is not self-indulgence, it is self-preservation, and that is an act of political warfare." Radical self-care.

Letter to Your Black Girl Self

The women in this chapter and others shared advice on stepping into your power. Write *two* letters. In one, share the advice you would give your younger self. In the second, offer the advice you want to remember five years from now.

EPILOGUE

PICK UP YOUR OYSTER KNIFE

I love you, Black girl.

I love Black girls in Afro puffs and Black girls in bundles of Remy.

I love the daddy's girls and the fatherless ones.

I love the little sisters who make straight As and the ones who skip school.

I love the hood girls and the suburban girls and the country girls, too.

I love the quiet girls and the loud girls—the lip smacking, smart talking ones.

I love the saved girls and the heathen ones.

I love the girls who stay in sweatshirts and Js and the ones in tight Fashion Nova 'fits.

I love the happy girls and the anxious girls and the girls battling depression.

I love the trans girls living defiantly.

I love the girls in the library and the ones on the basketball court.

I love the virgins and the young mamas.

I love the girly girls and butch girls.

I love the girls who fight.

I love the girls who love boys and the girls who love girls and the girls who love both or neither.

I love you, Black girl—unconditionally. (And whether you are fifteen or fifty.)

You hear me?

Today. I love you whether you look or act like "they" say you should. You are not wrong. And when you are wrong, I love you with all your flaws. No matter what choices and mistakes you have made. No matter where you live. No matter what you look like. No matter what thing has happened to you. And the greatest thing you can learn is to love yourself unconditionally, too. It may be the hardest thing you have to learn. I hope the letters in this book have shown you how.

One other thing, Black girl: you must learn to love other Black women and girls the same way. Love us whether we look or act like "they" say we should. We are not wrong. And when we are wrong, love us with all our flaws. No matter what choices and mistakes we have made. No matter where we live. No matter what we look like. No matter what thing has happened to us.

This does not mean you have to become a target for another Black girl's pain or anger or trauma. It doesn't mean you have to silence yourself in the face of Black women. It means you must give your sisters grace and understanding—the benefit of the doubt. So few people give us that; we owe it to each other. We have to acknowledge each other's humanity, even, maybe especially, when we are walking away. I hope the letters in this book have shown you how to do that, too.

Because we are sisters, Black girl. We have to take care of ourselves and each other.

You are me. I am you. We are alright.

Inside each of us are tiny pieces of our foremothers. Sarah Boone's ingenuity, Donyale Luna's unforgettable beauty, Toni Morrison's incomparable wisdom, Mamie Till's fierce love, Aretha Franklin's creativity, Marsha P. Johnson's fearlessness, Harriet Tubman's will to survive. Katherine Johnson's genius. Michelle Obama's grace. Black girls are made of all that magic, birthed in the African sun, baptized by the Middle Passage, and burnished by America. That is a power that no one else can claim. Just us.

We are sisters. You are me. I am you.

And we will get free together.

Zora Neale Hurston, a great Black woman writer, once said, "I do not weep at the world; I am too busy sharpening my oyster knife."[1] An oyster knife is a utensil used to crack open the shell of an oyster to get the tasty meat inside. Zora meant that she wasn't wasting time thinking about the hard parts of being Black and a woman, and she didn't care what other people said about her; she was busy trying to get at all the good stuff life had to offer.

Celebrate your Black girl life. Celebrate us.
Be like Zora.
Get that oyster, girl!

── *Know This* ──

SARAH BOONE, a Black woman from North Carolina, invented the ironing board in the 1800s.

ARETHA FRANKLIN, called "the Queen of Soul," was a singer, songwriter, pianist, and activist. As powerful at pop as she was at gospel, Aretha is perhaps best known for her song demanding "R.E.S.P.E.C.T." from her man.

KATHERINE JOHNSON was a mathematician whose calculations helped send man into space. She was profiled in the movie *Hidden Figures*.

MARSHA P. JOHNSON was an activist for lesbian, gay, bisexual, transgender, and queer people. A trans woman, she is credited with starting the 1969 Stonewall Uprising, a clash between New York City police officers and queer patrons at the Stonewall Inn that sparked the modern movement for LGBTQ rights.

DONYALE LUNA was the first Black supermodel, and in 1966 was the first African American to appear on the cover of *Vogue* fashion magazine.

THE MIDDLE PASSAGE was the route across the Atlantic Ocean taken by slavers carrying enslaved Africans to new lives in America. More than four million Black men and women died in the Middle Passage.

TONI MORRISON is one of the most important writers in literature. Her books about Black lives won several awards, including a Nobel Prize and a Pulitzer Prize. Her first book, *The Bluest Eye*, was about a girl named Pecola who is treated badly because of her dark skin, poverty, and family situation.

MICHELLE OBAMA is . . . you *know* who Michelle Obama is— my forever First (Black) Lady of the United States.

MAMIE TILL was the mother of Emmett Till, a fourteen-year-old Black boy who was brutally murdered by racists in Money, Mississippi, in the 1950s. Mamie decided to leave the coffin open at her son's funeral and allowed newspapers to take pictures of his terribly disfigured body. She said, "I wanted the world to see what they did to my baby." Her decision helped fuel the civil rights movement.

Born into slavery, **HARRIET TUBMAN** took an estimated thirteen trips on the Underground Railroad. Often called "Moses," Harriet also fought in the Civil War, liberating nearly one thousand men, women, and children during the Combahee River Raid.

THE LETTER WRITERS

Thank you for sharing your wisdom, your stories, your scars, and your love. This is how we love each other.

Celeste Williams	Sherry Thomas
"Luminous P. Jenkins"	"Big Sis E"
Dr. Carolyn Strong	Lisa Butler
Faith Adiele	Marcie Thomas
Tatjana Rebelle	Tara Turk-Haynes
Erika Nicole Kendall	Deidre Bounds
Phyllis "Seven" Harris	Minda Harts
LaShawnda Evette Crowe Storm	Dr. Rachel Talton
Adrianne Traylor	Nicole Jackson
Bailey Anderson	Dr. Aiesha Turman
Rochelle Riley	DeShong Perry
Rev. Brandee Mimitzraiem	Jamie Golden Nesbitt
Hannah Eko	Renée Alston
Deesha Philyaw	Aishah Shahidah Simmons

Patrice Grell Yursik

Dr. Tyffani Monford Dent

Ieasha Ramsay

Toya Smith

Folashade Kornegay

Robin Tillotson

Dr. Sarah Jackson

Twila Jones

Lynne Adrine

Keesha Dixon

Mary Calloway

NOTES

INTRODUCTION

1 MacKenzie Chakara, "From Preschool to Prison: The Criminalization of Black Girls," Center for American Progress, December 8, 2017, *https://www .americanprogress.org/issues/race/news/2017/12/08/443972/preschool-prison -criminalization-black-girls/*.

2 Erin Killeen, "The Increased Criminalization of African American Girls," *Georgetown Journal on Poverty Law & Policy*, April 17, 2019, *https://www.law .georgetown.edu/poverty-journal/blog/the-increased-criminalization-of-african -american-girls/*.

3 "Black Women and Sexual Assault," The National Center on Violence Against Women in the Black Community, October 2018, *https://ujimacommunity.org /wp-content/uploads/2018/12/Ujima-Womens-Violence-Stats-v7.4-1.pdf*.

4 "Dress Coded II: Protest, Progress and Power in D.C. Schools," National Women's Law Center, accessed May 27, 2020, *https://nwlc-ciw49tixgw5lbab.stack pathdns.com/wp-content/uploads/2019/09/final_nwlc_DressCodedII_Report.pdf*.

5 "Sex Trafficking's True Victims: Why Are Our Black Girls/Women So Vulnerable?"Grantmakers for Girls of Color, accessed June 10, 2020, *https://www .grantmakersforgirlsofcolor.org/resources-item/sex-traffickings-true-victims-black -girlswomen-vulnerable/*.

6 "Kodak Black Says Light-Skinned Women Are Easier to Break Down," BBC, July 3, 2017, *http://www.bbc.co.uk/newsbeat/article/40479291/kodak-black-says -light-skinned-women-are-easier-to-break-down*.

7 "The Plight of Black Girls & Women in America," African American Policy Forum, accessed June 18, 2020, *https://static1.squarespace.com/static /53f20d90e4b0b80451158d8c/t/5422de0ee4b080d53cf82554/1411571214756/Did -You-Know_Plight-of-Black-Women.pdf?irgwc=1&clickid=1yXUs20KoxyORS2w UxoMo3cjUkiVqRXhwzVVSwo&utm_medium=pp&utm_source=adgoal%20GmbH &utm_campaign=adgoal%20GmbH&channel=pp&subchannel=adgoal%20GmbH &source=adgoal%20GmbH*.

8   Rebecca Epstein, Jamilia J. Blake, and Thalia Gonzalez, *Girlhood Interrupted: The Erasure of Black Girls' Childhood*, Georgetown Law Center on Poverty and Inequality, 2017, accessed June 20, 2020, *https://www.law.georgetown.edu/poverty -inequality-center/wp-content/uploads/sites/14/2017/08/girlhood-interrupted.pdf*.

CHAPTER 1

1   Tamara Winfrey Harris, *The Sisters Are Alright: Changing the Broken Narrative of Black Women in America* (San Francisco: Berrett-Koehler Publishers, 2015), 123.

2   CaShawn Thompson, "CaShawn," Black History Untold, accessed June 20, 2020, *https://www.blkhistoryuntold.com/herstory/cashawn*.

3   "How the Creator of #BlackGirlMagic Got Erased from the Movement She Started," For Harriet, April 11, 2020, YouTube video, *https://www .youtube.com/watch?v=y2Ko-mgo1DU*.

4   Marian Wright Edelman, *The Measure of Our Success: A Letter to My Children and Yours* (New York: Harper Perennial, 1993).

CHAPTER 2

1   Andre Benjamin, Patrick L. Brown, Raymon Ameer Murray, Antwan Patton, and Rico Renard Wade, "So Fresh, So Clean," BMG Rights Management, Sony/ATV Music Publishing LLC, 2000.

CHAPTER 3

1   Sevn Thomas, Vory, NAV, Cash (XO), Brittany Coney, Blu June, Jahaan Sweet, Boi-1da, Jay-Z, and Beyoncé, "Friends," Roc Nation, Universal Music Group, Columbia Records, and Parkwood Entertainment, 2018.

CHAPTER 4

1   "One Third of Your Life Is Spent at Work," Gettysburg College, accessed May 25, 2020, *https://www.gettysburg.edu/news/stories?id=79db7b34-630c-4f49-ad32 -4ab9ea48e72b&pageTitle=1%2F3+of+your+life+is+spent+at+work*.

CHAPTER 5

1   Bryan Stevenson, *Just Mercy: A Story of Justice and Redemption* (London: One World, 2015).

2   R8DIO, Raphael Saadiq, and Solange, "Cranes in the Sky," Columbia Records, 2016.

EPILOGUE

1 Zora Neale Hurston, "How It Feels to Be Colored Me" (Massachusetts: American Roots, 2015). (Originally published in the magazine *The World Tomorrow* in 1928.)

ACKNOWLEDGMENTS

To my Black girl beta readers—Taylor, Peyton, Lauren, Kennedy, and Kya. Thank you for representing for your sisters and using your voices.

To Deesha, DeShong, Tasha, Carolyn, Tyffani, and Rochelle— y'all are the essence of Black girl magic and Black woman greatness. I am honored to know you. Thank you for your love and support.

To Shabnam Banerjee-McFarland, Neal Maillet, Jeevan Sivasubramaniam, and the team at Berrett-Koehler Publishers. Thank you for believing in my ideas and supporting me in unapologetically writing for Black women and girls.

INDEX

ABOUT THE AUTHOR

Tamara Winfrey Harris is a writer who specializes in the ever-evolving space where current events, politics, and pop culture intersect with race and gender. She says, "I want to be a story-teller of the black female experience and a truth-teller to all those folks who got us twisted—tangled up in racist and sexist lies. I want my writing to advocate for my sisters. We are better than alright. We are amazing."

Well-versed on a range of topics, including the Black Midwest, Beyoncé's feminism, Rachel Dolezal's white privilege, and the Black church and female sexuality, Tamara has been published in media outlets including *The New York Times*, *The Atlantic*, *Cosmopolitan*, *New York Magazine*, *Ebony*, the *American Prospect*, and *Ms.*

Tamara's first book, *The Sisters Are Alright: Changing the Broken Narrative of Black Women in America*, was published in 2015 by Berrett-Koehler Publishers. Called "a myth-busting portrait of black women in America," by the *Washington Post*, the book won the Phyllis Wheatley Award, IndieFab Award, Independent Publishers Living Now Award, and IPPY Award.

Tamara has also been called to share her analysis on media outlets, including NPR's *Weekend Edition* and Janet Mock's *So POPular!* on *MSNBC.com*, as well as university campuses nationwide, including Princeton University, Purdue University, and The Ohio State University.

A native of Gary, Indiana, and a graduate of Iowa State University, Tamara lives outside Indianapolis with her husband, LaMarl; dog, Jax; and cats, Jinx and Magick. Tamara is also the cofounder of the Black Women's Writing Society and a proud member of Alpha Kappa Alpha Sorority, Inc.

ABOUT THE COVER

There is artistry in Black girls' very being.

In the shades of our skin and the textures of our hair.

In the way our mouths caress syllables—how we can say a thing like no one else can.

In the way we dress up—how we can pick the best gold hoops from the discount bin, lay our baby hair just right, put on some white Nike Air Force Ones, and be fly as hell.

In the way we show up—scratching, surviving, marching, protecting, loving.

In the way we create—perform like Bey and Rih Rih, rap like Megan and Nicki, write like Angie Thomas and Octavia Butler, make art like LaShawnda Crowe Storm and Kara Walker.

Our natural creativity is why even when folks hate us, they try to jack our swag. And it is why the imitators can never be us.

I celebrate Black girl artistry in all its forms. It is my dream that every book I publish feature the creativity of other Black women. The cover of *Dear Black Girl: Letters from Your Sisters on Stepping into Your Power* was designed by Monica Ahanonu.

Monica is a freelance illustrator, working and living in Los Angeles. A graduate of USC's School of Cinematic Arts, she began her career at DreamWorks Animation before becoming a full-time freelance artist. Monica's work has been featured around the world at festivals such as Art Basel; through brands such as Adidas, Salvatore Ferragamo, and Red Table Talk; and in media, including *Afropunk.com*, which described Monica's style as "a little Bauhaus, a little Warhol, vector illustrations packed with personality, nostalgia, and pride. Work that honors Black creatives, be they fashion designers, music legends, or cultural icons. Expressive portraits that bring an extra dimension to each subject."

Thank you to this Black woman for lending her brilliance to this book. Follow Monica's work on Instagram at @Monica Ahanonu.

— *Know This* —

OCTAVIA BUTLER was a science fiction writer known for stories including *Kindred*, about a young Black woman who time travels between her modern life and a Maryland plantation during slavery. A literary legend, Butler won numerous awards during her lifetime, including the MacArthur Fellowship.

LASHAWNDA CROWE STORM is a mixed media artist, which means she uses lots of different materials, including bronze metal and textiles. Her work explores often-ignored people and issues, including race, gender, and mental health. She also addresses economic injustice through projects about safety and vacant properties. Her work, *The Lynch Quilts Project*, represents the effect of lynching and racial violence on America through community-stitched quilts. See more at *ReclaimingCommunity.com*.

ANGIE THOMAS wrote the popular book *The Hate U Give*, which was later turned into a film starring Amandla Stenberg, while still in college. She was inspired by recent murders of young Black men by police. The story follows a Black girl, attending a mostly white private school, who witnesses the shooting of a friend.

KARA WALKER is a visual artist whose work examines race, gender, violence, identity, and sexuality. She is known for bold installation art, including *Insurrection! (Our Tools Were Rudimentary, Yet We Pressed On)*.

Also by Tamara Winfrey Harris

The Sisters Are Alright

Changing the Broken Narrative of Black Women in America

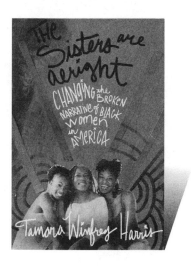

The Sisters Are Alright exposes anti-black-woman propaganda and shows how real black women are pushing back against distorted cartoon versions of themselves. When African women arrived on American shores, the three-headed hydra—servile Mammy, angry Sapphire, and lascivious Jezebel—followed close behind. In the '60s, the Matriarch, the unmarried baby machine leeching off the state, joined them. These stereotypes persist to this day. Emancipation may have happened more than 150 years ago, but America still won't let a sister be free from this coven of caricatures. Tamara Winfrey Harris delves into marriage, motherhood, health, sexuality, beauty, and more, taking sharp aim at pervasive stereotypes about black women. She counters warped prejudices with the straight-up truth about being a black woman in America. "We have facets like diamonds," she writes. "The trouble is the people who refuse to see us sparkling."

Paperback, ISBN 978-1-62656-351-3
PDF ebook, ISBN 978-1-62656-352-0
ePub ebook, ISBN 978-1-62656-353-7
Digital audio, ISBN 978-1-62656-651-4

Berrett–Koehler Publishers, Inc.
www.bkconnection.com

800.929.2929

Dear reader,

Thank you for picking up this book and welcome to the worldwide BK community! You're joining a special group of people who have come together to create positive change in their lives, organizations, and communities.

What's BK all about?

Our mission is to connect people and ideas to create a world that works for all.

Why? Our communities, organizations, and lives get bogged down by old paradigms of self-interest, exclusion, hierarchy, and privilege. But we believe that can change. That's why we seek the leading experts on these challenges—and share their actionable ideas with you.

A welcome gift

To help you get started, we'd like to offer you a **free copy** of one of our bestselling ebooks:

www.bkconnection.com/welcome

When you claim your **free ebook**, you'll also be subscribed to our blog.

Our freshest insights

Access the best new tools and ideas for leaders at all levels on our blog at ideas.bkconnection.com.

Sincerely,

Your friends at Berrett-Koehler